A Promise Kept
To Bear Witness

Joyce Wagner

Love
Joyce Wagner

Bloomington, IN   Milton Keynes, UK

authorHOUSE®

AuthorHouse™
1663 Liberty Drive, Suite 200
Bloomington, IN 47403
www.authorhouse.com
Phone: 1-800-839-8640

AuthorHouse™ UK Ltd.
500 Avebury Boulevard
Central Milton Keynes, MK9 2BE
www.authorhouse.co.uk
Phone: 08001974150

First published by AuthorHouse 4/27/2007

ISBN: 978-1-4259-9552-2 (sc)

Printed in the United States of America
Bloomington, Indiana

This book is printed on acid-free paper.

I dedicate this book with Love
In Memory of

-My Parents
Hersh Jacob and Gitel Witkowski

-My Eight Brothers and Sisters

-And My Husband Michael Wagner

Table of Contents

Acknowledgements ix

Forward xi

Radziejow 1

Family 5

Prelude to War 19

The German Invasion of Poland—1939 21

The Ghetto--1940 29

The Chelmno Death Camp 41

The Lojewo Work Camp—1942 45

Auschwitz-Birkenau--1943 61

The Death March--January 1945 91

Ravensbrueck 95

Mecklenburg 97

Liberation—1945 103

Back in Radziejow—1945 107

Back to Germany 111

United States—1949 115

Afterwards 127

Acknowledgements

Publishing these memoirs completes work that I started four years ago. During that time I was forced to re-visit many terrible events. Without the Love and Support of my family, this book would not have been completed.

I especially thank my grandchildren: Deena and Rachel Lipson, Brent, Brandon, Brittany Wagner and Michael Wagner, and Michael, Hilary and Eddie Ross~for asking all of the many questions, and listening patiently to the answers.

I thank my three children, Harold Wagner, Gilda Ross and Sally Lipson, and Dr. Paul Ross and Dr. Brian Lipson, for all of the encouragement given to me-- to not only tell my story, but to write everything down. The love of my children sustains me.

And special thanks to my daughter Sally for her patience in typing out my manuscript - and retyping and RE typing it—so many times over the past four years. Truly, I could not have done this without you.

A thank you to Dr. Rodney A. Ross of the National Archives for his interest in my project. His gentle and caring "prodding", and taped interviews he started doing with me thirty years ago were key in assisting me in getting my story down, and my book finally completed.

I also much appreciate Marci Kayne's editing expertise in reviewing and correcting my manuscript.

Finally, I need to thank the loved ones and friends who are no longer here, but whose presence I have continually felt as I revisited difficult memories. Sometimes I will wake from a dream where we are all sitting together, my lost family and I, and various members of my family and friends are trying to help me remember (and include) more stories about them in my book. I have searched my memory as best I can, so that they can live again through my words. I did the best job that I could. I love you all.

Forward

I am not a professional writer or speaker. I am a Holocaust survivor who wants to tell the story of what I lived and witnessed and lost during World War II.

Today, I speak of the promise I made to those who did not survive. I shared their suffering and inhumane treatment. Unlike other members of my family and so many millions of innocents, I avoided death in the gas chambers of Auschwitz/Birkenau. These gas chambers did more than take the life's breath of individuals; they exterminated a way of life for the Jews of Europe.

Like so many others I came from a close knit family. I was born in a small town in Poland, Radziejow, where family and friends shared happy occasions and losses together. Now, no one from that world remains. There are only shadows and ghosts of a long ago past.

I write now about the lives of my family and friends who should not be forgotten as if they had never existed.

We lived in Poland, a democratic country where the rules to be good to your neighbor and treat everyone as an equal were taught to us from the cradle. We lived by the Ten Commandments which God gave to us. And, we were treated worse than animals. Our lives had no meaning to Hitler's Nazi regime and his followers.

My belief is that those people had no belief in God and did not fear his punishment for their killing, cruelty and crimes.

I believe that every person is judged by God for their good deeds to humanity, and also punished for their inhuman behaviors.

For many years I have been asked by my children and grandchildren to write my story. This undertaking began as a very abbreviated paper about my immediate family and some of my experiences in the Holocaust. But this is a painful subject for me, and thus I first produced something that was extremely short. As I re-read my words and thought about the results of my initial efforts I came to realize why I was so unhappy with what I had recorded. My family members were more than just names; they were real people who were a part of my life. Each family member was an individual human being who was tortured and killed so early in life.

So I started over, and that is how this book came to be. This undertaking has been burdened by a crushing sense of responsibility. It is a memorial to those who did not survive.

The Holocaust was something that should never be forgotten. It was an event unparalleled in human history. It went beyond human imagination. But I was there.

How could this have happened in a civilized world? It is unbelievable. I tell the story of what can occur when the world is silent and lets a tragedy like this happen.

Six years of my own youth were wiped away by those awful events to be replaced by nightmares of tragedy, misery and death. To this day I still cannot believe that it all even happened; that my eyes witnessed those horrors and that I lived these experiences.

These words were not easy to write. The pages of this book are stained by many tears. But now, in reading over the finished manuscript, I feel satisfaction for what I have accomplished. I have kept a promise that I made to my friends in Birkenau and have created a living testimony for my family. Future generations of my family will re-live these events through my words and my testimony.

In my mind, everything that happened is fresh, vivid and new. Like it all happened yesterday-or today. It is a dream. It is a nightmare. But remember. Above all else remember, that every word is real. And these words combine to form me: one Holocaust survivor. The words document a world that no longer exists – the great, rich, thriving tradition that was European Jewry before World War II.

Those Holocaust victims are now gone, except for what lives on in the memories of the remaining, few survivors. Mine is a big story for one person. Mine was but one family among the lost six million. My story is woven from the fabric of real people-of flesh and blood. It is MY story, the story of Joyce Witkowski Wagner.

Come now and see and live through my mind and heart. And remember the Jewish people and the other victims who were murdered in the Holocaust. Remember my experience and its message of hope and tolerance of others.

CHAPTER I

RADZIEJOW

I was born in a small town in Poland called Radziejow Kuj. The total population was probably about five thousand, and of this number the Jewish population was approximately one thousand people, with the first Jewish inhabitants having arrived there five hundred years earlier. The majority of the Jewish population was middle class and self employed. They were skilled craftsmen and business people.

We had a strong Jewish identity, and the town had an active Jewish life. Radziejow had its own Jewish library, Jewish bank, Jewish theatre, and Zionist youth movement. (Zionist organizations supported the founding of a separate Jewish State). Zionist groups that I remember from my childhood were Hashomer Hatsair and Betar.

Some members of our Zionist youth actually immigrated to Palestine in 1935.

I met some of these friends from my childhood on my visit to Israel at a Holocaust Survivors Convention in 1967, just before the onset of the Israeli "Six Day War." These people expressed deep regret to me that more of the youth of Radziejow did not follow them to Israel, in that most of those who stayed behind eventually were to perish in the Holocaust. Those few who left Poland in 1935 were the only survivors of their own large families.

Education and study of Torah has always been valued by the Jewish people, and my hometown was no exception to this fact. In our small town we had two synagogues, a religious school for boys, and a Beit Yakov, which was the school for girls. There also was a private teacher by the name of Rabbi Zaif, who was my mother's teacher, and instructor of other Jewish children.

While I was growing up, much of the rest of the world, even the world that surrounded our small Polish town had modern appliances, automobiles and airplanes. But in the Radziejow of my childhood, life went on as it had for centuries of simpler times.

Streets were cobble stoned, and horses were used for transportation of people and goods. There was a private bus that was used to transport people from town to town, and a few wealthy people owned cars. I recall the town doctor making his daily rounds, riding in a handsome horse and buggy, as he visited his patients. For most everyone else, bicycles (or walking) were the common mode of transportation.

No one in our community had ice boxes or refrigerators. Instead, a cellar was used to keep perishables cool. There were no electric appliances, but we did use electric lights. Our family utilized a wood burning oven to keep us warm in the winter. My mother cooked our meals using a wood burning stove.

Judaism and family were the center of daily life. We kept a Kosher home. The Sabbath was the sacred day of rest.

Traditions were important in the Jewish community of Radziejow.

Some weddings were performed outside of the Temple, and then, in the absence of buses and limousines, people would walk to the home where the wedding celebration would take place. I recall one particular wedding where the groom's family and the groom's guests walked from the home to the town square, and then to the hall for the ceremony. There was singing and dancing in the streets (an orchestra accompanied them!) as the groom's family welcomed the bride, her family, and guests at the wedding reception. There were no limousines to transport the wedding party.

A sweet event such as this wedding helped the flavor of the beautiful way of life that existed in my town.

People did not "barter" for goods and services. Currency was utilized, just as it is in our world of today. Yet in most other ways, how the people of my youth lived would be difficult for my own children and grandchildren—those who have grown up accustomed to the everyday and immediate access to television, computers, cellular telephones, and video games.

And yet this way of life was very real, and a very typical home for many of the six million who died in the Holocaust.

This was my life in Poland, as a child and a young teenager. It was a way of life that was very simple, and in its simplicity and its family and Jewish values and traditions, it led to a happy childhood.

Built on a mountain, Radziejow was surrounded by more mountains and valleys. The main business center was in the town square and surrounding streets. In the evenings we would walk around the square, meeting people and friends, conversing on all kinds of topics, books we had read, town happenings or events of the world. We would stop in a cafe for some coffee or tea, and enjoy a piece of cake or share a piece of chocolate.

In the winter we had fun sliding down the hills on homemade sleds. Sometimes we had the luxury of a ride on a sled drawn by horses.

On Sundays in the summer we would walk to the mountains. Then we would go on through the woods on our way to the farmers where we would enjoy refreshments consisting of a piece of hot black bread with lots of butter, washed down with cold sour milk (like a yogurt). I still hold the taste of this special treat in my memory.

After resting there for a while I would return home from an enjoyable journey with our friends. The mountain valleys contained orchards where we could buy fresh fruit from the gardeners which we enjoyed very much.

My family lived a comfortable life. Even with nine children there was always plenty to eat in the house. My mother saw to it that we were nicely dressed, always sharing our clothes. We had a "live-in" who took care of us because my mother had to spend time helping out in our family store.

We had lots of cousins to play with. We were a close-knit family that lived very close to each other and celebrated special occasions together.

Life in Radziejow was simple, peaceful and enjoyable.

CHAPTER 2

FAMILY

I came from a loving family with eleven members, comprised of my parents and nine siblings. I was the second oldest of the children.

The first of the children was my brother Meyer, a tall and skinny boy who was both smart and athletic, with a beautiful singing voice. His athletic skills were proven with a medal he had won as the best runner in school.

When Meyer was fourteen, he contracted typhus during an epidemic in our town. My father took him to a hospital in Wloclawek, a big city, hoping to get better care for him there. His hospital room-mate was a friend named Aaron Frankenberg. These two boys passed the time by singing. They would sing all kinds of songs so much so that when Dr. Fuks walked into their room he would remark, "Is this a hospital or a concert hall." We always wondered if the stress and strain of all of this singing may have worked to weaken Meyer and worsen his condition. Two days after being admitted to the hospital, Meyer died. His friend Aaron survived

I too contracted typhus in that same epidemic and was a patient in that same hospital in Wloclawek. My younger sister Hava who also had typhus was successfully treated at home. Fortunately we both recovered from that terrible disease which claimed the lives of my brother and many friends and schoolmates. The typhus epidemic truly devastated our town.

After Meyer and I, the next child in our family was my brother Schlomo. He was very good in his Hebrew classes and very religious and studious. My father was very proud that his son was so beautifully following his example as a student of Jewish studies. Schlomo could always be found using every free minute studying the Talmud (the Bible and its oral interpretations). Had he survived the Holocaust, he might well have studied in a Yashiva (a seminary training school for Rabbis). Schlomo was a perfectionist. Using an iron that was filled with hot coals, he would insure that his pants were always perfectly pressed, and that he was flawlessly dressed.

Next in line was my brother Bernard with whom I shared a very special relationship. He was the love of my life.

Bernard was very smart, and very loyal, always standing up for me. In addition, he was extremely generous, sharing any and all treats with me. He worked very hard with my father and the other helpers in our family bakery. Bernard would labor all night to have the bread and rolls baked fresh for our morning customers. Many people of our town did not have their own ovens for making baked goods, and they would come to our bakery to use our ovens for baking their own cake or cookies.

They appreciated Bernard's baking efforts, and he would receive tips from the customers. He would always share some of his earning with me, so that I could buy myself extra little things, personal items, like lipstick. I loved spending time with my favorite brother, and often I would break dates with my friends just to go on walks with him. Bernard kept unusual hours, working at night in the bakery, and then sleeping during the day.

Bernard suffered through two serious illnesses. At the age of ten he contracted an infection that spread to his brain and his chances of survival were slim. Yet by a miracle he not only survived, but made a complete and total recovery, coming home to rejoin the family after two months in the hospital.

A second crisis for my brother occurred in 1940 when a terrible tooth infection spread to his chest. He was taken care of by a Jewish doctor, Dr. Sheinberg, a cousin of ours. Dr. Sheinberg ran away from Gdansk after he was not allowed to practice or take-care of patients anymore because of the Nazi invasion.

Dr. Sheinberg put me in charge of cleaning and bandaging my brother's infections. He called me the best nurse he ever had. Bernard's condition continued to worsen and he was taken to a hospital in Aleksandrow. This happened after the Nazi-German invasion of Poland. He remained in the hospital for two weeks, recovered, and was sent home. The day after his discharge, all of the sick Jews were taken from that hospital and shot by the Gestapo.

The fifth of my siblings was a brother, Abram. I remember that he was a very beautiful baby. Abram became ill from diphtheria, developed a high temperature, and passed away when he was only two years old.

The sixth was my brother Shymek. He was the youngest of the boys and was very lovable. Quiet and bashful, Shymek was a lover of animals. He adored baby ducks, and raised them in our backyard. He would feed them, and provided a big pan of water where they could swim.

I can see Shymek and the ducks in my minds eye running and playing together in the yard, having great fun together. One day someone left the fence door open and the ducks all disappeared. Shymek was heartbroken; he missed them so much.

The seventh of the children was Hilda. Being the most quiet of all of the siblings, she would be the last served at the Friday night dinner table, but she never complained. She was the one who was deported with my brother Shymek and me to Auschwitz.

Next came my sister Haya, a smart and pretty girl who took good care of her baby sister Hava. She was always protecting Hava, sharing her toys, and playing nicely with her.

When Haya was about three years old she developed a bad habit of sucking her fingers. To get her to stop my mother made her a little blanket as a distraction which she then carried with her as a constant companion for a long time.

The ninth child was Hava, the baby of the family, and the most adorable child with her smart, childish remarks. She was such a happy child. She was very pretty and got the most attention from her older brothers and sisters.

All of my brothers and sisters got along very nicely, and we had so much fun playing together.

We had a little garden in our backyard where we planted our favorite vegetables. I remember that our carrots never seemed to get too big—we ate them when they were still little and sweet. We also had a little space in the backyard where we loved to roast potatoes. The crispier they were, the better they tasted.

At other times, on weekends, when we were off from school we could be found sitting around the kitchen table. My father would begin measuring and cutting from a large roll of paper. These paper pieces eventually became bags, not only for our store but for other businesses also. My mother would mix a paste of glue to place on the bottoms of the bags. The children would then fold them together to complete the process. It was a fun project for the entire family. I can still see their smiling faces as we all worked together.

We loved each other and were protective of each other. The older children (including myself) had the responsibility for helping the younger ones with their homework.

My mother and father were very protective of their children.

When I returned home from the hospital after recovering from typhus that it was the last night of Chanukah. My father was lighting the eighth candle, but no one was singing the Chanukah songs that I loved and was so used to hearing at that holiday. When I asked my father why he wasn't singing, his reply was, "I have a sore throat, but I promise that at your wedding I will sing many beautiful songs." The next morning when I walked down to our store one of our customers told me how sorry she was that my brother Meyer had passed away. I didn't even know that I had lost my brother Meyer to the epidemic. When I heard that I was so shocked! My parents could not bring themselves to tell me this horrible news.

My mother, Gitel Poczczywy Witkowski, came from a business-type family. She was a hardworking woman who was devoted to her husband and children. She taught us the value of education and honesty, and the importance of getting along with others. She loved us with all of her heart.

I remember that during my brother Bernard's illness, my mother was told by Dr. Fuks that it would cost lots of money to save Bernard's life. Her response was, "I have a house. I will sell it and save my child."

The expenses of treating Bernard's illness were tremendous. We lost that house and saved my brother.

My mother was also very charitable. When there were some poor people passing through our town, the men from the synagogue had to find them a place to eat. Often it would be with our family. My mother would say, "Where there is food to feed my family, there has to be more for one or two more hungry people."

My father, Hersh Jacob Witkowski, came from a rabbinical family. He was highly educated, and possessed a beautiful singing voice. My father went to synagogue twice daily, and had a special way of harmonizing with, and enhancing the prayers that were sung during the services. He delighted the entire congregation with his chanting of prayers. The women of the congregation were especially appreciative of the way he beautified the services. They called my father the best "Baltifilla" or service leader, and thanked him by saying, "Yasher koach Reb Hersh Jacob."

My father was always dressed nicely in his long black coat with his red beard. He looked very distinguished. He was an Orthodox Jew. At home, we always said the appropriate blessings before and after meals, and observed all of the Jewish holidays. On Saturdays our family store would be closed for Shabbat, and in the afternoons my father would study the Talmud. He was a good hearted person who would not think of coming home from synagogue without an "orech", a poor person, to join our family for dinner.

My father was a very generous man, and was an active member of the synagogue's congregation.

Once I recall that my father was going around our town with Rabbi Platkiewicz, collecting money for some of the poor. When they entered our store my youngest sister Hava began to speak to my father in Polish. The Rabbi was greatly surprised by this because most of the religious Jewish people spoke Yiddish in their homes. The Rabbi asked my father, "How come you speak Polish in your house?" My father's answer was, "My children had a problem with the Polish language when they started school, so I allow some of the Polish language to be spoken in my home."

My father was a religious man yet he still tended towards some modern ways of life.

A different memory demonstrates my father's commitment to the laws of Judaism. One Saturday afternoon one of my friends came over to our house and brought a mandolin. We went into the living room and closed the door so that we would not be disturbed by the other children. My friend played his mandolin, and when my father walked by the room he heard the music. He softly knocked on the door, walked in and said, "Children, today is Shabbat and you are not allowed to play a musical instrument on Shabbat." He closed the door and walked away.

In my mind I can still see the gentle look he had on his face when all of this happened. My father was a very religious Orthodox Jew, and always a gentleman.

Another Shabbat story from long ago was when we had finished our special meal, and I went out for a walk with my friend, Yetta. We were soon joined by a third friend, a young man who was home on vacation from school. As we walked along together, our student companion took out a cigarette, lit it, and began to smoke. I reminded him politely that it was Shabbat and that because of this he should not be smoking. He ignored my remark. I said again that while he was in my company he should not smoke on the Sabbath. He then stated that we were "old fashioned." At that, Yetta and I left him and walked away.

When we returned home my father asked why we had taken such a short walk. When we explained what had happened he assured us that we had done the right thing and that he was very proud of us for using good sense.

My father was a very understanding parent and he trusted me. One evening, after completing my work in our family store, I felt like taking a walk around the town square. As I left the store I noticed our gentile, next door neighbor standing on the steps of his house. He asked if he could join me. He did and we walked the town square together, having a lovely conversation. Little did I know that this innocent stroll would start people gossiping. The next day some members of the Jewish community approached my father and told him that they had seen me out walking with my neighbor. My father answered, "He is just a neighbor, and I trust my daughter. She knows what is right and what is wrong."

That was what life was like in a small town where everyone knew everyone else. And that was my father: very religious and very strict, and yet understanding of life's situations. He was always there to protect us and to provide guidance.

My father had served in the army during World War I, and I remember him telling us a story about his homecoming at the end of his military duties. When he returned to his home, he found that his mother had put out clothes for him to wear—and that these were the same "traditional" clothes he had previously worn as a student studying to become a rabbi. (My father's grandfather was also a rabbi). My father refused to dress this way, telling his mother that he wanted to be a businessman so that he didn't have to live on handouts; the way some of the small town Rabbis lived in Poland.

We celebrated many happy occasions together. My brothers' Bar Mitzvahs were truly special events. We had a ceremony at the temple where the service was performed, welcoming a new member into the adult male Jewish community. Then we would return to our home for a Kiddush for family and friends together with plenty of food and the singing of religious songs. In those days, a Bar Mitzvah was judged by the performance of the young man being initiated into Jewish adulthood and not by the quality of the party that was held later, a situation that is often reversed today. My brothers all distinguished themselves with outstanding performances at the temple.

In Orthodox Judaism girls do not have Bat Mitzvahs. Some families would even favor sons over daughters. In my family my father loved his girls and my mother loved her boys. Still, we felt we were loved by our parents equally.

We also celebrated many birthday parties. Birthdays always were associated with a special Jewish holiday – and that is how we would remember them. One was either born just before, during, or just after a given holiday.

For example, my birthday was on Succoth which is a harvest festival. My family would celebrate the occasion in our lovely decorated Succah—with branches for its roof and fruits hanging down in celebration of the harvest. Children would work busily, making paper cut outs and strings of chestnuts to hang from the roof of the Succah. This was a happy holiday, and made for a happy birthday remembrance for me. Families would gather together in the Succah for dinner and every wife would put forth her best efforts to prepare the most special recipes for the family, as did my own mother.

Chanukah was another lovely holiday. We lit candles for eight sacred nights, and sang songs to commemorate the miracle of the oil that burned in the temple for eight days during the long ago time of Judah Macabee. The soldiers fought the Greek army and expelled them from the Jewish land, and took over the Holy Temple in Jerusalem. On Chanukah we ate special potato pancakes fried in oil, called "latkes." The children would receive toys (most of them handmade), or a penny for Chanukah gelt (which we would then save in our little homemade wallets which closed with a purse draw-string).

Passover, the Jewish festival of freedom, was another happy occasion. We had to carefully clean our entire house to remove any and all bread products, and then prepare a Seder, a ceremonial meal, with plenty of Passover food. The children would always receive new clothes for Passover, so they could look their best at the Temple. We ate matzo and sang Passover songs. Our family would always try to host a lonely person for the Passover Seder.

Yom Kippur, the Day of Atonement and the holiest day of the Jewish calendar, was another most memorable holiday. I will never forget the special family ritual that accompanied this most sacred day. After our meal that preceded the 25 hour fast of Yom Kippur, my father would bless all of his children, going in order from the oldest to the youngest. With tears streaming down his face he would ask God's blessing, and pray for the safety and protection of the children who he loved above all else. Then we would leave for Kol Nidre services. Yom Kippur was the most solemn of holidays where we, along with Jews around the world, prayed on the sacred Day of Atonement.

Friday night was also a special time. My mother would be busy cooking all day for the Friday night and Saturday meals. She would put out the white tablecloth and set the table. At sunset, she would light the Shabbat candles and say the prayer. All the children had to wash up and dress for the dinner.

After my father returned home from temple with my brothers, and sometimes an orech (a poor man), he made the Kiddush (a prayer for wine), we washed our hands and said a prayer over the challah (egg bread), and then we had our special festival meal with songs.

All of our holidays meant a great deal to the whole family, especially to the children.

Many of these holidays were spent with extended family and friends. I have many good memories of those days.

My father had two brothers and one sister. One of his brothers, Vigdor, immigrated to Palestine as a Zionist pioneer in 1933. His brother, Moshe, and sister, Tziprah, were murdered in the Holocaust along with their large families.

My grandmother Bella was a sick woman who had already passed away when I was a little girl. My grandfather Aaron Joseph Witkowski was sent with his family, and my mother's family, and my younger brother Bernard to Chelmno, a death camp. It was in that horrible place that this family was wiped out as they met their ends being gassed and buried in the Chelmno woods with thousands of others.

My mother had three brothers and three sisters. Two of my mother's brothers, Max and Sam Levy, immigrated to the United States in 1904. This family's youngest sibling, a brother named Israel, immigrated to the United States in 1938 along with his wife and three children. They were among the lucky ones. If they had stayed in Poland just one additional year, their fate would have been the same as those who were left behind: death in the Nazi concentration camps.

My Uncles Sam and Max sent papers that would have allowed my parents and siblings to immigrate to America also. But my father did not want to leave his own parents behind. He made all kinds of excuses why he couldn't take his family out of Poland and relocate in the United States. My mother never forgave him for that; she wanted so badly to get out of Poland.

My Aunt Hilda, my mother's sister who had twelve children, died as a young woman. Two of her sons, my cousins, immigrated to the United States; one in 1922 and the other in 1930. Another of Aunt Hilda's children, Ben Neuman, survived the Holocaust and came to America in 1948. My other two Aunts on my mother's side of the family, my Aunts Rivka and Aunt Hava, were murdered in the Holocaust along with all of their large families.

I remember my maternal grandmother on my mother's side, Grandma Miriam Leizerovich Poczczywy, very specifically. She was a very clean woman who always wore three aprons one on top of the next. One apron was for cleaning the house, one apron was for business, and one apron was for going out.

Grandma Miriam was also a very generous woman, always trying to help others. When a poor young woman planned to get married and there was no money in her own family for the wedding, my Grandmother Miriam would go out to collect donations so that the bride could have a nice wedding. She even wrote her two sons who were living in America, Max and Sam Levy, for money to help others who were less fortunate.

Grandma Miriam visited her family in the United States in 1935. After two years in America she returned to Poland. She wanted to be buried next to her husband. She passed away naturally and peacefully in 1940 and was put to rest as she wished. Her husband, my maternal grandfather Bereck Poczczywy had passed away when I was a little girl. Unfortunately, I do not remember him.

My parents owned a "general store" where groceries could be purchased. In addition, many other items were part of the inventory; paints, clothes, sugar, coffee (and the cups to drink it in) to mention only a few. This was a "mom and pop" type of store where the whole family worked in the business. We were well know in our small town of Radziejow and all sorts of people, Jews and Gentiles, would shop there. We saw townspeople; teachers, church fathers, and farmers as customers.

Our store was located between two churches. The stores were forced to close on Sundays, and those who tried to conduct business as usual on the Christian holy day were fined.

As a small girl I enjoyed helping my parents in running their business. I would stay at the counter, doing my homework, and at the same time waiting on customers. My friends came into the store after school to buy candy and I was their saleslady. I felt so important. It felt good. When the wholesale salesmen came into the shop so that we could order goods they would always bring me a toy thinking that I would then give them a larger order of merchandise.

I attended school until I was fourteen years old. Jewish students had bible classes (taught by the Rabbi and his daughter) while the Christian students had their own separate Bible studies taught by a Catholic priest. The German language was another part of the curriculum that was required.

After my day at public school I would go to the school for Jewish girls, Beit Yakov, where I received my formal Jewish education.

It is vivid in my memory, a one week trip I took with my religious school class to the town of Wloclawek. My teacher was from this town and it was quite a beautiful trip. Wloclawek was a big city located near the Wisla River. It was an industrial and cultured city, with a university and many libraries. It was so different from Radziejow—it had large buildings, the finest restaurants and theaters, hospitals, and many cars. It had lovely shops stocked with the latest fashions.

We formed a group of about forty girls, and we stayed in our teacher's house. We slept on blankets on the floor. It was like a pajama party, but also educational. During the day we visited the city's special education centers and picnicked on the banks of the Wisla River. Before bedtime we had our study class. All in all it was a beautiful week and holds a wonderful memory of lots of fun!

I will never forget my graduation day. My classmates and I were performing for parents, family, and friends. We were dancing and singing with streamers hanging from our wrists. We all sang in Polish,

"How swiftly time flies away. In a day, in a year we won't be together."
It was both a happy and a sad celebration, not knowing what the future
held for any of us.

There was no college in our town of Radziejow, nor was there any
university near by. With nine children it was impossible to consider
sending one of us away to continue with higher education.

For a time, I belonged to a Zionist Organization called Hashomer
Hatzair. My father was opposed to my continuing as a member of
this group because it was a socialist/Zionist organization and among
other discussions, I learned about sex education which was against
my parents' wishes. This was the only "sex education" that I ever
received. Eventually my father made me drop out of Hashomer
Hatzair.

As a young girl I loved reading books, and I enjoyed working at
the library. Books allowed me to travel to exotic far away places using
the power of my imagination.

After graduation I went on holiday to visit my father's family in
the town of Isbice. I had a lovely time on this trip. I made lots of
new friends, went for walks in the beautiful countryside and swam in
picturesque lakes.

The image is still fresh of one vacation long ago. The year was
1938 and there were rumors that Poland would soon be at war with
Germany. I visited a girlfriend in Sompolno, and made many new
friends, both boys and girls, who were beautiful people. I remember
this so vividly. We had the most, lovely time.

One Saturday night there, a male friend asked me to go for a walk
with him. We were dressed alike. I was wearing a white skirt and a
navy jacket and he was wearing white slacks and a navy jacket. There
was a troop of performers putting on a show, and some children
noticed us walking by and thinking we were part of the performance,
they excitedly gathered around us to talk. When I think about these
young people, so full of life, all from wonderful families like mine, it
is just heartbreaking. Those cities, Isbice and Sompolno, were not
too far from the Chelmno extermination camps and I think the Jews
who lived there were among the first to be deported to Chelmno.

Later, after the end of World War II, as I searched for family and friends, I was unable to locate a single survivor of these two towns.

Soon after graduation I went to work in my parent's store. Since I was the oldest of the children (with the passing of my older brother Meyer) I gradually took over the responsibility for running the store. I recall when we had a demonstration in our store for the product Jell-O. Several salesmen had come from America, and they brought in large pots to cook the Jell-O in. The people from our town came to taste this new item. I quickly learned how to mix the flavors, and we had a Jell-O party at our house soon after that for all of my friends to experience this new treat.

As an older teenager I began to become active in both the library and the theatre. Very often my friends and I would be chosen to serve as ushers in the theatre. We would wear white embroidered aprons, and had the responsibility for seating people and serving refreshments. It was an honor I so enjoyed.

I spent time with both Polish and Jewish friends. I also enjoyed learning how to play the mandolin, and knew many Polish and Jewish songs.

Jews and non-Jews got along well. Life was peaceful despite the fact that some of the Polish people were antisemitic.

On one occasion I got to know some of those antisemites. We had a Jewish soccer team in our town and the Jewish boys would play against the Polish team. Games would take place on Sundays in a small village not far from our town. The Polish people would cheer for their team and the Jewish people cheered for the Jewish team. At one game I remember the Jewish boys were playing well and were winning. Some of the Poles started a fight. There were many more Poles and they started chasing Jews. I was one of those Jews who felt that I was running for my very life! We heard the Poles shouting "Kill the Jews!" and other antisemitic words. Some of my Jewish friends who could not run fast were caught and beaten. The police came (later!) and dispersed the crowd. It was a very scary incident. Some of the antisemitism of the Poles was exposed in this episode.

I also recall the man who delivered water from the well to our houses. He went around singing in Polish, "Our street, your houses... the land belongs to us."

The Jewish boys felt these hostile feelings more than the girls, and often fights would break out due to their sense of being discriminated against.

I remember my mother recalling an incident that had occurred in our store. She was waiting upon a nicely dressed gentleman who had come into the shop to buy a large pot for boiling potatoes for the workers on his farm. He remarked to my mother "I am so happy to have found a gentile business." My mother was so nervous that my father would suddenly walk in dressed in his traditional Chasidic clothes!

Thus it was that we Jews came to understand prejudice and hatred that was directed at us from some anti-Semitic, Poles of our town.

CHAPTER 3

PRELUDE TO WAR

From 1933 to 1939 we were all disturbed by bad news coming out of Germany. Polish Jews who lived in Germany were deported back to Poland. Some German Jews were escaping to Poland, and these new arrivals brought reports of what had been happening in Germany as a Nazi State under the leadership of Adolf Hitler. Hitler had come to power in 1933. We listened, horrified, to stories of the burning of books written by Jewish authors, of the deportation of people to camps, of hard forced labor, of the closing of schools to Jewish students and other unimaginable events.

In the beginning it was hard to believe these descriptions, but after awhile we realized that we were being told the truth.

Then came Kristallnacht—the "night of the broken glass" –on November 9, 1938. The windows of Jewish homes and Jewish owned businesses were smashed by German Brown Shirts and Gestapo. Jewish properties were destroyed, synagogues were burned to the ground, and many innocent Jews were murdered by the Nazis.

There was no room for Jewish people in Hitler's Germany.

Some people from our town left, escaping to Palestine, Australia or America. Others didn't believe that these awful stories of German antisemitism could touch those of us who lived in Poland. These people assumed, unhappily and incorrectly, that Germany would not invade Poland, and that Jews were still "safe" in the Polish homeland.

Meanwhile, my Uncle Israel Levy, Auntie Manya, and their three children (Marlene, Bernard and Nathan) immigrated to America, and that was when my parents took over their bakery. Our business location was relocated to the site of that bakery.

Later after the German invasion of Poland the street of the bakery became part of a Jewish Ghetto.

CHAPTER 4

THE GERMAN INVASION OF POLAND—1939

I vividly remember September 1, 1939. It was a beautiful fall day and I was listening to the radio playing in a neighbor's window while working in my parent's store. The program was interrupted with the announcement that Germany had invaded Poland!

This was a very sad day for all of us.

We knew that Germany had plans to invade Poland, and in preparation the Polish government had recalled troops to strengthen its army. We were even instructed in the use of gas masks, fearing that the Germans might use poison gas against the Polish people. We had meetings in our town on how to best prepare ourselves in case of an invasion.

Poland was a small country with a small army poised to defend itself against an enormous and powerful German force.

When the German planes began their bombardment of Polish cities we had no idea what would happen next. We heard some shooting and saw the smoke from fires burning not far from our town.

Much of the population of Radziejow panicked, and started running away to get farther from the German border.

We took a horse and wagon and my six siblings and I (without our parents) followed other refugees down the road to another small town, Osieczyny Kuj. The roads were crowded with horses and wagons, heaped to the top with personal possessions and food. My younger siblings were unaware of the reason for our trip. They were having fun singing and laughing and enjoying the ride.

Jews and Poles were pushing and shoving forward, trying to escape the approaching German Army. Occasionally we saw Polish soldiers traveling every which way; confusion was all about us. My father had been born in Osieczyny Kuj, and had some friends there. When we arrived, the people of this town looked at us like we were crazy. The Weisman family opened their home to us, as we would later for other people after the establishment of the Ghetto. I stayed there with my brothers and sisters for two days. On the first night the children were tucked in at bedtime but it was impossible to close our eyes. Bombings and shootings were going on throughout the night.

In the morning, German soldiers were in the streets of Osieczyny. We then realized there was no point of attempting to run further. The Germans were waging a type of war they called "blitzkrieg" and were rushing across Poland. There was no way that we could outrun them. The German troops had already taken the town of Osieczyny. I felt there was nothing to do but go back home. So we packed our things and returned to our home in Radziejow.

In a few short days the Polish army was in full retreat, and in two weeks the Germans had complete control of Poland. I lost some close friends in this war, both Jews and non-Jews.

German soldiers occupied our town, but in the beginning these soldiers didn't immediately bother with us. Soon afterwards things began to change, and rapidly, for the worse.

The German Army now had complete control of Poland. Still, we had a family store to run, and needed supplies for our customers. I went to the wholesale market in Wloclawek to purchase groceries for the store. I traveled on a bus loaded with people, and didn't encounter any problems with German soldiers on the trip out. When we arrived in Wloclawek, we went to a relative's house, and she cooked dinner for us. After the meal we relaxed and talked about what the future might hold for us.

Suddenly, a group of black uniformed Gestapo, the German secret police, burst into the house searching for men to put to forced labor, and took some away. One of the Gestapo looked at me suspiciously, touched my chin with his whip and walked out. After they left I burst into tears. I was so scared, afraid that the Gestapo might come back looking for me. So, we left that house immediately and found another place to stay. We all had experienced our first taste of the Gestapo.

The next morning I went to the wholesale marketplace, and when the Jewish owner saw me, he told me that I was crazy for making the trip. His store had been broken into and he had been robbed of all of his supplies. His shelves were all empty! Life in Wloclawek was changed in horrible ways. People were being selected for work details by the Germans, and then they would just vanish. So we quickly left Wloclawek and returned to Radziejow.

When I arrived home the occupying German Army forces were evacuating the area, and the Gestapo was moving in. They took over the city administration building for their headquarters. My father felt a responsibility to our customers and tried hard to keep the store open and the bakery operating. We thought, we hoped, that with the passage of time, conditions would improve.

One day we went to pick up some flour for the bakery. I went to a Polish man who owned a mill. Driving back home with our flour, we passed a German "Volksdeutsche", a German national who was living in Poland, who also owned a flour mill. He reported me to the Gestapo because I had conducted business with the Pole instead of him! The Gestapo came to the store and ordered me out! They took me to their headquarters to be interrogated. After being questioned they let me go. This incident left us all terrified. What was next? We didn't have long to wait to find out.

German Volksdeutsche came to the store, selected merchandise, and told us to deliver it to their homes without paying for it! The

Germans now felt that everything that the Jews of Poland possessed belonged to them.

That was when Hell on earth started for us.

Shortly after the invasion, Hitler issued a law that all Jews would be required to wear a yellow Star of David on their clothing—front and back.

Jewish men cut off their beards so they would not be subjected to the cruelty and humiliations of the Gestapo.

Jews were forced to walk in the streets, and were forbidden to use the sidewalks. Some of the Poles looked on with indifference as these acts of malice were committed against the Jews.

It was not only the Jews who were targeted by the Gestapo. The Gestapo took all of the Polish intelligentsia, including teachers and priests, and put them in detention centers for political prisoners. The Germans feared that educated Poles could lead a revolt.

Schools were closed.

Jews were put to work doing degrading tasks like street sweeping, washing sidewalks and performing housekeeping chores for the Gestapo and Volksdeutsche.

We felt so humiliated.

Jews were overworked and beaten. The Jews were slaves of the Gestapo who could do whatever they wanted to us. Even commit murder. We were totally helpless.

Then the Gestapo struck again, ordering the closure of all Jewish owned businesses. A seal was placed on the door of our store to ensure that we would not remove any merchandise. Jews were given the smallest amounts of food which were carefully rationed but it was not enough to live on. We were literally starving in our own homes!

In desperation one of our neighbors worked out a method of removing the seal from our store and then restoring it so that it would not be noticeable. This allowed us to access some goods which we later exchanged with some Poles for food. This helped us to survive. Of course doing this meant taking a life or death chance. If we had been caught, we all would have been shot.

Stores and homes of all Jews were now being ransacked by the Gestapo.

They also went into two beautiful churches and two beautiful synagogues and removed all items of value, sending everything off to Germany. A few weeks later the Gestapo burned our synagogues. Then they assembled all of the Jews of Radziejow in the town square and searched everyone for matches thereby attempting to blame us for the arson committed to our own synagogues. We later heard stories about how in other towns Jews were hanged or shot for allegedly burning down their own synagogues.

Early in 1940 the Gestapo assembled all Jewish males in the town square and began deportations to forced labor camps. My father and my brother Schlomo, along with many others, were sent off to build streets and lay railroad track. These slave laborers were given only the smallest amounts of food to sustain their efforts. Of course the "soup" was non-kosher, so some of the religious men had to live only on tiny rations of bread.

The work was extremely hard, and some became ill from malnourishment and abuse. After several months of this torment my father and some of the other older Jewish males were sent back home. These men had serious injuries and were literally "skin and bones."

My brother Schlomo and other young Jews were sent to Pozen prison camp. We never heard from them again.

Jewish women were sent by the Gestapo to work details near the town of Inowroclow. I was assigned to a group of girls and our work consisted of the demolition of buildings and then the cleaning of bricks so they could be used for other construction projects. This was a deserted place where the Polish Army previously had a training center but now, had no use for the buildings. This work was very hard labor. We would sit all day in the sun, cleaning bricks, covered with dust that was so thick that we could barely see. When the wind would blow, the dust would swirl about and we could hardly breathe. When we didn't work as fast as our foremen demanded, we would be beaten with clubs. We were watched by Volksdeutsche foremen.

We received meager rations and at night were forced to sleep on concrete floor covered with some remnants of straw.

Some of the girls would also be sent to clean the houses of the foremen. I was sent once and recall that the German foreman had a beautiful young wife, three small children and a very large home. I wasn't done with the cleaning until late in the evening, and then had to be back and ready by early morning to march out to my daily work.

Another day I was selected by the same foreman to accompany him and take measurements of a large building. I imagined that I had probably been picked because I knew German, having learned this language at school. I couldn't have been more wrong!

I was told that this particular building was going to be fixed-up for some offices to be used by the German Government officials. So we drove together in a car to Inowroclow. As we passed an airport he stopped the car to show me the airplanes. It was kind, but strange that he would do that. When we arrived at the building site we found it to be empty and abandoned. Straw was strewn about where some German troops had slept. We started taking measurements and then I realized that this foreman had other plans for me.

He approached me and made advances. He promised that if I did as I was told he would give me a pass to return home for a week. My answer was that he had his own beautiful wife and that it was "rassenschande", absolutely forbidden, for a German to have contact with a Jewish girl. "Why are you doing this?" I demanded. In response he told me that he is a man and "rassenschande" does not mean anything to him. Scared, I was standing there and tried to convince him to leave me alone. We started arguing back and forth while he came closer and closer toward me. I started backing up and then ran from him. He began to chase me through the empty rooms. When I got to the entrance door, I escaped outside. For a moment, I stood there afraid for my life and I realized that he could have shot me for running away. He came right out after me and told me to get back into the car, and he drove me back to the work camp.

I call this scary incident one of my miracles.

Several times after that, this German foreman would choose other girls to go with him on "measuring" trips, and they all received passes to go home for a week. I was the only one who knew the real reason for this "generosity." I never mentioned the incident to anyone.

Close to our work camp there was another group of Jewish girls who worked in the fields of a German farmer. We waved to each other but never had any real contact. We never even found out where these girls were from. After a few months when the work in the fields was completed they were sent away. We all had a bad feeling for what had happened to them. Were they sent home or to another work camp? Or were they sent to their deaths?

We had heard so much bad news about the cruelty of the Nazi German regime. We were soon to experience more of this cruelty first hand.

In mid 1940, Hitler ordered that Jews were to be isolated in ghettos, and that they would not be allowed to have contact with any members of the outside world.

The isolation of the Jewish people, prelude to extermination, had begun.

CHAPTER 5

THE GHETTO--1940

After my initial work camp experience, the brick cleaning project, was completed we were all sent home.

Home was now the ghetto where all of the Jewish people of Radziejow had been segregated onto one street. Before the German occupation, some Jews had previously lived in nice/well built homes on one of Radziejow's streets we called the "Yiddisha-gahs" (the Jewish street). Now, all of the Jews were concentrated by force into this one street.

Over two hundred families were crowded into this designated ghetto area. Four families were now living in our house, eight adults and over 20 children, packed in under one roof. The over-crowding was unbelievable. We all had to share the kitchen, which was also "the bedroom" for one of these families.

The Gestapo came to the ghetto every day and selected Jews to clean the streets or work at other tasks of hard labor.

One day they picked my brother Bernard to go off together with other chosen Jews to work on a German farm. We thought we would never see him again, but at night he returned with the group. He was exhausted and had been severely beaten, but at least we had him back.

Every ghetto had a certain number of members of the Jewish community who were called "Judenroth," who would function as "go betweens" between the Gestapo and the Jews of the ghetto, and Radziejow ghetto was no different. Some members of the Jedenroth worked hard to better the status of the ghetto Jews.

We lived in constant fear of the Gestapo. When you saw them coming you knew you had to immediately hide. Do anything to stay out of their way. I remember another incident where the Gestapo came to the ghetto, and were conducting a door by door search, looking for young people to be taken to forced labor. I was ill in bed suffering from a high fever. It was winter in Poland and we didn't have any fuel with which to heat the house, so it was very cold. My mother was really scared that they would just snatch me out of bed, high fever and all, and send me away. So she got me out of bed and quickly hid me in a shack in our backyard. The Gestapo came to our house and because they could not find any young people to take, they did some random damage before they left.

The German people and the Gestapo took advantage of any free labor they could force from the Jews. They brought material to Jewish tailors who then had to sew for them. Suitcase makers had to construct suitcases with which they could then send their stolen plunder back to Germany. The Germans who owned farms came down to the ghetto to pick out people to work for them.

We Jews were seen as nothing more than a slave labor force to be used and then discarded when individuals became too sick or weak to continue working.

Often the Gestapo would come to collect Jews from the ghetto to take to the town's market square. There they separated the women from the men. The women would go off on a forced march for many miles until they would reach some German farms where we would then be forced to dig for potatoes or harvest other vegetables. The Jewish males would be taken to perform some hard labor task, like ditch digging. This was going on in the summer. In the winter months, we were forced to shovel the snow from the streets. Receiving only the smallest rations of food to sustain our efforts we often felt that we simply did not have the energy to continue these labors. The Gestapo was literally working us to death. We had no choice but to follow the orders to survive, or be shot.

Curfew time in the ghetto was five o'clock at night, and we were strictly forbidden to be out of our homes after that deadline passed. We had no telephones but we young people still found a way to communicate with each other. We made holes in the backyard fences so that we could crawl back and forth between houses to see each other.

Of course Jews were forbidden to listen to the radio. All radio devices were confiscated early in the German occupation by the Gestapo. So we got information on what was going on in the world by the oldest method of all: "mouth to mouth."

We ghetto Jews did not receive any rations of soap with which to keep ourselves clean so we made our own. All electric service to the ghetto was shut down so one of our neighbors made kerosene lamps by which we lit our houses at night.

Food provided to the Jews was strictly limited and we had very little to eat. People were starving. Getting more food meant leaving the ghetto though it was forbidden, and required removing our yellow Star of David from our clothing to go out and find some food to survive.

Confined to the area of the Radziejow ghetto, and with both of our synagogues having been burned, people would gather in secret to pray in private homes. Schools had been closed, and the education of Jews was forbidden, so teachers would gather children, perhaps five in a group, to secretly continue their educations.

Jews were making every effort to maintain their dignity, and keep life as "normal" as possible under horrendous conditions.

Before the burning of our synagogue, an attempt was made to save the Torah Scrolls. Jews of the ghetto had five or six beautiful old Torah Scrolls still in their possession. Some of these scrolls had been given to our community by a wealthy family from Warsaw, the Mazers, whose father had served as a rabbi in Radziejow at the turn of the century. In 1935 members of the family returned and built a beautiful synagogue and donated Torah Scrolls as a memorial to their father. After the Germans isolated all of the Radziejow Jews in the ghetto we hid the scrolls in different homes. Afraid that these hiding places were not safe, they were then moved again and hidden in the ovens of our old bakery – in ovens that had been used prior to the War for the baking of Passover matzo, but which had been closed down since the German occupation.

A day came when the Gestapo ordered all of the Jews of the ghetto from their homes and assembled us all in the market square. They then went through our houses looking for any hidden items of value that could be sent back to Germany. They stole as they wished and committed random acts of vandalism as they left.

I will never forget that particular day—it is so vivid in my memory. It was on a Saturday, and it was a beautiful sunny day. We all stood together in the square and talked about what would be next. What would be our newest punishment? After several hours of our forced assembly in the town square we were released and ordered to return to our homes. We were absolutely stunned to find our beautiful torah scrolls torn to shreds and spread out onto the street for us to walk upon.

These were the same holy scrolls for which, during Temple services we would stand in respect. Now they were being walked on. We had hoped that we could hide them and save them, but sadly the Gestapo had discovered them, desecrated them, destroyed them, and used them as a tool to further humiliate the Jews of the ghetto. We were devastated and demoralized. Our precious Torah Scrolls were lost to us.

We always worried about our survival. Would we have enough food to last another day? Would we be selected for hard labor, removed by force from those we loved, and never be seen or heard from again, as had already happened with my brother Schlomo? Or would we survive this nightmare? Would we be evicted from our homes? How long would this all last? We went on with the process of living, but with so many questions. When would this time served in Hell end?

After living in the ghetto for a few months we felt like animals locked up in a cage. Food was scant. People were on edge and on each other's nerves, health deteriorated. How long could this go on?!

Again, some people tried to run away to save their lives. Some ran to the Russian border and temporarily escaped. Some returned to be with their families and died together. Others were killed in Russia when the Germans launched their eastern front and invaded the Soviet Union on June 22, 1941. A few of those who escaped to Russia somehow traveled all of the way to Palestine. Some who had survived the war in Russia eventually returned to Poland after the war to search for family members.

By the end of 1941, Germany occupied almost all of Europe. On December 11, 1941, the United States declared war against Germany.

Some people ran away deeper into Poland toward the Czechoslovak border—we called this the "protectorate." There were rumors people would be protected there, that they might be used in exchange for German prisoners. We wanted to believe this was true. Therefore, my parents and my two youngest sisters, Hava, age 10, and Haya, age 11, left with whatever valuables we still had, and went to Klobuck, a city close to Czestochowa, hoping they would survive there.

My younger sister Hava did not want to go. She wanted to stay with me because my plans were for my two brothers, Bernard and Shymek, my sister Hilda, and I, who were all older and still able to work, to go to a nearby work camp for Jewish people. Hava was crying and holding on to me and said, "I don't want to go away. I want to go with you." This was an awful experience for me. She cried, "You want to live, I want to live too. In the working camp, as long as I can work I will stay alive."

I convinced her that this was impossible because of her age. Unfortunately, the German Nazis had no use for children. In the protectorate, she would also have a chance to survive. My father put on a farmer's straw hat, some baggy work clothes and with his red hair he looked like a farmer. My sisters had light colored hair and with my mother covering her head with a scarf, they looked like peasants.

When my mother was leaving the train at Klobuck, she was looking to see if there was any Gestapo around, frightened that they would be recognized as Jews. Sometimes the Gestapo were searching for Jewish people and if they were caught, they were taken off the train and shot. In the commotion, she missed a step, fell down and broke her leg.

Now I would risk my own life by removing my yellow Star of David and going by the train to visit my parents and sisters and bring them some food. As the oldest of the children I knew that they needed help. That it was my duty to try and help, in any way that I could. Though I knew that it was "forbidden" for Jews to leave the Radziejow ghetto, that it was "forbidden" to remove the Star of David, and that it was "forbidden" for Jews to use the trains, I still needed to try. Many things were forbidden to Jews at that time, and the penalty for a violation of the rules was deportation to a concentration camp, or immediate death. But I did these things anyway.

I walked for an hour to reach the train station with my packages. I was wearing a full skirt and a white blouse, and had my head covered with a handkerchief. In this disguise I looked just like an ordinary peasant girl. On the train I kept my face hidden in a book, and nobody paid the slightest bit of attention to me. I was lucky with my light colored hair and upturned Polish-styled nose, I could feel a little more secure. Despite all of that, when I was sitting on the train, I still did not feel safe in my disguise. Every time I saw a Gestapo walking the aisles of the train I was terrified. I was so scared of them that I would push my face even deeper in the book I was pretending to read. When I arrived in Klobuck there were so many German soldiers around the platform that I could easily slip off the train and away from the station without being detected.

Was I the brave one? Or, did I do these things for the great love I had for my family?

When I saw my mother on the straw on the floor, my tears began to flow. What a terrible situation she was in! She was in pain and could not walk. How would she ever be able to care for my father and two small children!?

The conditions in Klobuck were unbelievable. There were many families packed together, living in this huge warehouse. There was no privacy and there was little food. I met some other families from Radziejow who had traveled there with their own small children, distressed refugees, trying to get to Czestochowa to the imagined safety of "the protectorate".

Everything was dissolving into chaos and confusion. There was absolutely no logic to what was going on. Families from other parts of Poland were "escaping" to my town of Radziejow, thinking that they would be safer there, somehow, then their own persecuted Polish villages. People from our town, knowing that it wasn't safe in our ghetto, ran to the protectorate with the hope of survival. It was a time of utter madness. I returned home to Radziejow.

I was unable to get the picture out of my mind, of my sick mother laying on the straw and the way my family lived in Klobuck. For the second time I risked my life, took off the yellow Star of David and made the trip to see my parents and sisters. I brought them some more food and tried to find another, better, place for them to stay. But the situation was so difficult in that town; everyone else was also searching for a "better place to stay". It was not possible to find other living quarters for my family. Klobuck was just too overcrowded with refugees.

I looked at my father's skinny face. He had lost so much weight, he looked terrible. I looked at my mother lying there on the straw with her broken leg. Then I looked at my baby sisters. They were just children. In their faces I could read so many questions that had no answers, "Why did you send us here to this Hell away from our home? Away from our friends who we used to play with? Away from our own beds where we happily slept?" I felt guilty at that moment that I had not done the right thing in allowing our family to be separated in this way. But I hoped that they would find safety in the "protectorate." I wanted them to have the best chance for survival.

My family was happy to see me, but all were worried about my taking such a risk in traveling to see them. They all made me promise to be careful. I assured them that I would take every precaution, and would try and come to see them again.

In those awful conditions, my parents and sisters continued to live in the Klobuck warehouse. My father was very worried about the rest of his children—the separated members of the family who were still back home in Radziejow. He asked me repeatedly if I had heard from my brother Schlomo who had been sent to work in the prison of Posen. My father pleaded with me to try to help Schlomo. I assured him that I would try, but knew in my heart that what he asked of me was impossible. I would never be able to reach the Posen prison, let alone be able to see or assist my brother. Posen prison was like a black hole. No one knew what the conditions were like for those Jews who had been sent there, or if they were even still alive. So I returned again to my brothers and sister in Radziejow, my promise to my father unfulfilled. I never imagined that this would be the last time I would see my mother, father and two younger sisters alive.

By January of 1942, Hitler and his chief operators ordered the "Final Solution of the Jewish question", the destruction of the Jews of Europe, which later became known as "the Holocaust."

We heard awful rumors of what was happening in other towns. Jewish people were being taken out of their homes and taken into the woods to be shot, and others sent away never to be heard from again.

Some other townspeople didn't believe what Hitler's Nazi regime planned for the final solution, the killing of all of the Jewish people. A neighbor of mine questioned me about sending my parents and younger sisters away to the horrible conditions that existed in the protectorate. As if I had any control over what my own parents would decide to do on their own! Or that I would ever have "planned" for the division of my own family. I felt even more lonely. Already, I missed my family so much.

In the beginning of the summer of 1942, for a third time, at great risk, I planned to set out to Klobuck to see my parents and sisters again. I prepared in the evening for a morning departure, but I never made it.

At daybreak the ghetto was awakened by the voices of the Gestapo screaming "**JUDEN RAUS! JEWS, OUT OF YOUR HOUSES**

NOW!" There were the loud barks of vicious dogs, and there was pounding on doors. The Gestapo was closing down the ghetto!

We had all expected that eventually something like this would happen and that death would now be our fate. We Jews had lived in fear of the "final solution", but all around us there was still denial. Some townspeople didn't believe in the stories of what the Nazi regime had planned – the total and complete murder of all of the Jews in Europe.

With this raid at early dawn the Gestapo caught everyone in the Radziejow ghetto completely by surprise. Whole families were captured. No one was prepared. And the next day, all were gone. A whole town of Jews, with a heritage that stretched back through many generations and hundreds of years had vanished.

Expecting something like this to happen, my brothers Bernard and Shymek, sister Hilda and I had previously made emergency plans to hide with a neighbor in our adjoining attics. An opening had been made between them so that we could move between houses undetected.

When we heard the Gestapo screaming "ROUSE!" and the barking of the dogs we grabbed our coats, threw them on over our pajamas, and ran for the attic to hide. A group of us quickly and quietly gathered there: Moshe Frankenberg and his wife Schprintze (the older sister of the man who would later become my own husband), their daughter (and my girlfriend) Yetta, and their three other daughters Salla, Dorrie and Genya. All of us huddled together in this hiding place.

Two members of the Gestapo entered the attic to search for hiding Jews. We scrunched down behind the chimney of our bakery. Lights flashed about as they looked around the attic, but they couldn't see us. We were lucky, because if they had brought their dogs up with them we would have never escaped detection. Those trained dogs would have sniffed us out and our capture would have been quick. But there were no dogs. They satisfied themselves that no one was there, and they left.

Then a terrible thing happened. My brother Bernard panicked and ran from the attic down to the basement to hide. He thought that somehow he would be safer there. A Gestapo discovered him in his new hiding place and took him away.

That was the last time I saw my brother Bernard.

Meanwhile—another near disaster was in the making. Another Gestapo had found the concealed attic door on the neighbor's side of our connecting homes, and began screaming "JUDEN RAUS!" He entered our hiding place, and the first girl he encountered was Salle, someone he knew. This girl's father was a suitcase maker. This particular Gestapo had previously brought over the materials for the construction of suitcases that would later be used for Nazi plunder being sent back to Germany. She pleaded with him to spare our lives. She begged him to just leave us there in the attic. "We will come down later" she said. He stared at us, and then he sympathized with us. He spared us. He left the attic, went down and out the door and nailed it shut.

"Niemand ist hier", I heard him tell another Gestapo-no one is here.

To this day I cannot believe what happened in that attic, and how lucky we all were. After witnessing so much random cruelty and murder at the hands of the Gestapo, here we were all saved by this one Gestapo.

Huddled together in the attic we heard all sorts of things going on in the streets. There was shouting and screaming, dogs were barking, and shots were being fired. People were screaming out the names of loved ones. In all of the confusion and despair, families still wanted to be together. Some people tried to run for their lives, but all were caught and shot.

The Jews who had been captured, including my brother Bernard, my Grandfather Joseph and other family members, were all ordered to the market square, the whole of the Jewish ghetto of Radziejow.

All were herded by the Gestapo into a church overnight. A friend of mine named Alex somehow managed to hide in the chimney of that church and survived. Much later he told me how he had unsuccessfully begged my brother Bernard to hide there with him. Bernard was tired of running, hiding and living in misery. He just gave up. To this day I wish that he had not given up so easily. He was older than my brother Shymek, more mature, and he was a good organizer. With these skills he might have had a chance to survive.

I would later find out through Alex details of that terrible night in the church. The conditions were unbelievable. People received nothing in the way of food or water. People had been evicted from their homes so swiftly by the Gestapo raid that no one had time to take along provisions. Some Jews watched as family members who tried to flee were gunned down. People were crying. No one knew what to expect....what was coming next. Young couples with small children were desperately begging for food and water, of which there was none. So the Jews of the Radziejow ghetto stayed locked in that church for a day and a night.

Thinking as we hid in that attic, I was relieved that my father, mother and two sisters were in Klobuck. I was sad that we were now separated, but at the same time I realized that had they stayed in Radziejow they would now be locked in that church. Had my parents stayed in Radziejow, likely all of our family would have been caught together in the dawn Gestapo raid, and would now be locked up together in that church. And all of us would have been deported together to the Chelmno Death Camp.

CHAPTER 6

THE CHELMNO DEATH CAMP

In the morning the Gestapo removed all of the Jews from the church, loaded them onto trucks, and drove everyone to the extermination camp in Chelmno, named for its closest local village. This was Germany's first extermination camp that used poisonous gas where half of a million Jewish people were murdered.

Jews from Polish towns surrounding Radziejow were also being transported to Chelmno. We learned that when they arrived, Jews were ordered to remove all clothing for "showers"—being told that after this, they would be sent to work camps in Germany. The Jews were then loaded onto specially constructed vans, the doors were shut tight and the poisonous gas was poured in. All the people in the vans were thus murdered. It was a horrible death by suffocation. Then the bodies of the victims were taken to the Chelmno woods where they were stripped of their jewelry and dumped into huge mass graves.

Some Jews in Radziejow did find out early what happened in Chelmno. A German man who was friendly with a Jewish tailor named Grabski had traveled to Chelmno and although he was not allowed in, he learned the news from the guard, as one Nazi to another, how the Jewish people were killed there by gassing. The other Jewish people thought these words were only rumors which they did not want to believe. They could not imagine that a place like that existed in the twentieth century. They refused to accept such terrible news.

The nine of us huddled in that attic, on the day of the Gestapo raid on the Radziejow ghetto, were terrified. We did not feel at all safe, fearing that the Gestapo who initially spared us would change his mind and send some of his fellows to drag us down from our hiding place. So as soon as it was dark, we left the attic and ran towards a slave labor camp which was not too far from our town.

One of our Polish neighbors saw us fleeing and immediately reported us to the Gestapo. We hid in a haystack in a field, and thanks to God, they were unable to find us. Thinking back on it now, I have this sense that the Gestapo member who was sent after us might well have been the same man who had saved our lives in the attic, and that he didn't make a very serious attempt in his search for us. We were all very lucky to escape.

I call this, another of my miracles.

At daybreak we left our hiding place and did a head count to insure that we were all still together. We heard shouting coming from the direction of Radziejow. At that time the Gestapo were loading Jews onto trucks that were bound for Chelmno.

We continued on through the fields and farms, trying to get as far away from Radziejow, keeping low so that we would not be seen by any Poles or Volksdeutsche. As we finally approached the working camp, we knew that we were safe for awhile.

Back in Radziejow my brother Bernard wasn't so lucky. He was one of the Jewish prisoners being loaded on those transport trucks headed to the Chelmno death camp. Bernard had made a terrible/ wrong decision when he ran down to that basement and none of us would dare stop him. It happened so suddenly and at that time we did not know which area was safer, the basement or the attic.

Instead of the four of us, we suddenly had only three siblings left. Bernard had always been such a big help trying to protect us and working hard to insure that there was sufficient food in our house. I missed him so much. My brother was such a special and caring person, and he did not survive. It wasn't easy to let go.

It still isn't easy.

The woman who had reported us to the Gestapo when we first left the attic was a single mother with ten children of her own. She had made a living before the war working for Jewish neighbors, and we had helped her and her children. We felt sorry for the children, and they were our playmates. And yet when this woman saw us running for our lives she immediately reported us to the Gestapo.

Every nationality has good and bad people.

Some people saved their Jewish neighbors because they had good hearts. Some risked their lives to save Jews. Some saved Jews if there was money to be made. And some people turned Jews into the Gestapo to be killed.

Growing up in Radziejow, I learned to distrust the intentions of some of the Polish people towards the Jews. Some Polish people could be very nice, while others were antisemitic. Jews knew who they were but were careful to hide any negative feelings that they may have had about these neighbors.

I witnessed and lived through many antisemitic incidents prior to the onset of the German occupation. Most of these incidents were unpleasant but still tolerable. Jews tried hard to live in peace alongside of their Polish neighbors. I truly believe that without Hitler's invasion of Poland, my extended family could well still be happily living in Poland. But that was not to be.

Some Polish people needed an instigator to openly display their feelings, and Hitler was their answer. Some Poles collaborated with the Nazis in the persecution of the Jews.

The Nazis chose Poland to be the site of the slaughter of the Jews of Europe. It was in Poland that they constructed the worst of the extermination camps. I do not blame all of the Polish people, just the bad ones. Some Polish friends later cried with me when they learned of the fate of their Jewish neighbors.

CHAPTER 7

THE LOJEWO WORK CAMP— 1942

When our little group arrived at the Lojewo Work Camp all of the Jews there were deeply saddened by the news of what had happened to our families and friends in Radziejow. Together we mourned all of the rest of the day. People were openly sobbing and no one ate or drank. It felt like a religious fast day that was full of mourning.

None of us knew what fate had in store for us. And as to our family and friends– we had the strong sense that we would never see them again.

But this was a work camp, and life had to go on. We all had to return to hard labor if we were to survive a little longer. The work camp provided meager rations, and we had to eat in order to live.

At Lojewo we were housed in big barns, with separate quarters for the women and men. Our work was the construction of streets, and this required pulling heavy wagons piled high with stones. This work was exhausting and debilitating, but no one was going to miss a day of labor, even if he or she were sick.

We were closely watched by German Volksdeutsche and Polish foremen. Some of us also worked as tailors. Food was tightly rationed. A little sugar or butter was considered the most outrageous luxury.

We wore the clothes that we had brought with us during our escape to the work camp. We kept ourselves clean. Every few weeks we would be taken to a bath house where we took hot showers. Every Sunday, on our day off from work, we washed our clothes in a nearby river.

We were free to walk to visit Polish farmers who lived near Lojewo and some of them became friendly with us. But we did have certain restrictions. We were not allowed to venture out too far from our work camp.

Once, one of my co-workers went on an unapproved visit to see a relative in a work camp not far from ours. He was caught and murdered by the Gestapo.

After I was settled at the work camp, I wrote a letter to my parents. I did not mention any details about the fate of my brother Bernard. I just could not send my mother and father more bad news. I knew that they were already grieving for the loss of many family members. I only wrote that we had escaped in our pajamas and that we were safe, but that we had been unable to take anything else with us.

My mother sent me some embroidered tablecloths which I was to use to make dresses for my sister and myself. I had a good friend at the Lojewo work camp who had been a dressmaker, and she helped me with the sewing. We had no other possessions than the clothes on our backs.

The other men and women at the Lojewo camp had been allowed to bring clothes and money with them. Yes, they worked every bit as hard as my siblings and I, but they were still more comfortable. With their money they were able to purchase extra food from the nearby farmers. Since my sister Hilda, brother Shymek, and I had come to the work camp in only pajamas and our coats, we were miserable. We had to depend on the generosity of other workers to share some of their clothes with us. I felt like a beggar. Life became so degrading. I couldn't live that way on handouts.

I was so desperate that I took a big risk to improve our conditions. My plan was to return to Radziejow where a month earlier all Jews had been rounded up and deported to Chelmno death camp. I was hoping to get help from some of my Polish friends. I promised our camp foreman, a man named Urbanski that I would bring back some medicine from our Polish druggist who had been friendly with my family, if he would give me some papers stating that I was sent to buy some medicine for the camp. It was a very risky undertaking.

For the first mile of my trip home to Radziejow I was accompanied by a close friend named Jacob who tried hard to convince me not to go. He pointed out that I was taking a big chance and might well be caught by the Gestapo. But his arguments fell on deaf ears. My mind was made up and I would not turn back. We kissed good bye, and he returned to the Lojewo work camp.

Thinking back on those events, I wonder if I had listened and returned with him to the camp if things would have worked out differently. Perhaps he would have had a better chance of survival. But I was young and a risk taker and I was determined to see my plan through to its completion.

I reached Radziejow without incident and went immediately to the house of a Polish friend who put me up for the night. This also was very risky. In the morning I walked out to the street where I had lived so happily with my family.

It was strange and horrible, like a bad dream. The street looked like a ghost town. The doors of the houses were all closed. Windows were closed. Where there used to be so much life, where children played and neighbors gathered to talk, now there was nothing. No sounds at all. Nobody was left in my old vibrant neighborhood. All were gone.

I went to the home of a former customer of ours, a German Volksdeutsche named Lange. She cried with me over the tragedy of what had happened to my family, as well as the sad fate of other Jews from the Radziejow ghetto who had been sent to Chelmno to be gassed.

Then her husband arrived, and he was so surprised and happy to see me. He openly encouraged his wife to help me. Things were going so well, and then their thirteen year old son returned home unexpectedly dressed in the uniform of the Hitler youth. Lange quickly hid me in a closet, afraid that her son would turn me in to the Gestapo. The young couple who were brought up among Jewish people felt sorry for me but their young son who was taught hatred in the Hitler youth group would turn me in. When he left, I came out of the closet relieved that he did not see me. She gave me some cooking oil from their factory and some ration cards for bread. I felt like a beggar. Then we said our goodbyes and she wished me good luck. I stopped by the pharmacist with the letter.

How could I have done this? The pharmacy was only a few steps away from the Gestapo headquarters. The druggist was even afraid that I would be seen in his drugstore. He gave me some medication for the camp and quickly let me out through the back door.

Finally, I returned to my house and crawled inside through a back window. Everything was exactly as it had been when I had left. It was sad going through the empty rooms that were filled with so many memories. I picked up some clothes and money – money that I would later use to buy extra provisions of food from Polish farmers near the Lojewo work camp. For reasons unknown, I felt like a thief, despite the fact that I was taking my own things from my own home. Tears filled my eyes as I quickly and quietly left the house.

I had to hide my supplies on my body and that wasn't an easy task. As I left Radziejow I had to carefully watch my every step. I realized that there was enormous danger that some of my former Polish neighbors could still recognize me and turn me in to the Gestapo. I was lucky. I left the town unnoticed, and set out to return to Lojewo.

As I walked back to the work camp I was met by a Volksdeutsche who owned a big farm and who had been a customer of ours before the war. After the German invasion of Poland he took advantage of the available/free Jewish slave labor, and treated those who worked for him badly. He recognized me when he saw me and asked what I was doing in the vicinity of Radziejow, when all the Jews from the ghetto had been deported. I explained that I had come to purchase medicine for the work camp and that I had papers. He didn't know what to do with me, whether to turn me in to the Gestapo or let me go. Then he said: "I liked your father. He was a good Jew." Perhaps at that moment his mind was drifting back to pleasant memories of the delicious egg bread that he picked up every Sunday from our bakery. My father used to take special care of him and treated him nicely. He looked me over, and then let me return to the camp. But there was a moment, as we stood there together and he decided my fate, when I thought I wasn't going to make it. I call that incident another of my miracles (and good luck).

On my return to the camp everyone was happy to see me back safely. They appreciated the medicine that I brought back with me because medicine was so limited in the working camp.

It looked like bad news followed us all the time during Hitler's regime. After a few months, coming home from a hard working day, we got another runaway from Klobuck with the bad news that the Jewish people there were all rounded up and sent away to Treblinka, which was not a working camp but a death camp. I learned with shock and horror that my mother, father, two sisters and a few other people from Radziejow were on that transport. The people from the protectorate in Czestochowa, where they were supposed to be safe, were also liquidated and sent to Treblinka.

It was another tragic day for us. My sister, brother and I were devastated by the loss of our parents and two younger sisters. We cried our hearts out and tried to console each other over our loss.

Unfortunately there was no safe place for the Jewish people of Poland and other European countries. The Jewish people were put to death for no other reason than being Jewish and their belief in God. It was a systematic destruction of all Jewish people.

I found out after liberation what happened at the death camp of Treblinka where almost 900,000 Jewish people were murdered. People arriving there were told that they were at a transit camp on the way to be resettled. This was one of the many lies told to minimize resistance. Immediately upon arriving the men were separated from the women and children. Those too sick to walk were taken by a wagon to a pit and shot. My mother with her broken leg was one of them. My father and two sisters were taken separately to the gas chambers. The dead bodies were searched for hidden valuables and placed in mass graves. Their thoughts as they were crowded into the gas chamber smelling the gas haunts me to this day.

After working in Lojewo for awhile, a smaller group of us was sent to a smaller work camp not too far away. It was a big farm in a beautiful country side not too far away from a small town, Broniewo. Our living quarters were a big house with separate areas for men and women. They provided us with plenty of food. We did not receive too much bread but a thick soup with plenty of fresh vegetables and horse meat. The work was very hard, supervised by the farmer's helpers and our Polish foreman. We worked in the fields, and when that work was done, we cleaned canals, drained ditches and built small bridges in the cold winter weather without boots.

One day when we were working in the fields, we encountered a big storm with thunder and lightning. The only place to hide from the bad weather was under some trees or under a big wagon. I went with others and hid under a tree. My sister and another group took cover under a wagon. Then I heard my sister calling that it was dangerous to be under the tree during the lightning so I joined her group under the wagon which saved my life. One of the men, a schoolmate of mine, hid under the tree and when lightning struck, he was killed instantly. We lost a good friend and we gave him a funeral attended by other workers from nearby working camps.

This incident, like others, is so buried in my mind after so many years, that when I hear lightning and thunder today, I still get very scared.

After working at this small camp for a few months, we were again ordered to return to the large work camp Lojewo. We were all frightened because we heard about Hitler's orders to liquidate all Jews—to make Europe "Judenrein"—purified of all Jews. We did not know what to expect. We were all young, still able to work, and loved life too much. To be sentenced to death was beyond our imagination.

Some of us gathered outside the building, questioning what could we do. We felt we didn't want to go to slaughter like sheep. Revolt? With what? Protecting ourselves with the only weapons we had, our shovels, was ridiculous against the Gestapo with their guns. We would all be shot on the spot and there was no place to go, no place to hide. We were in a very bad and sad situation with nobody to help us and no means to protect ourselves. We had no choice but to stay there, wait, and hope for the best.

When I needed a knife to cut some bread and asked a coworker for one, nobody would give it to me because they were afraid I would commit suicide.

Life in the Lojewo work camp was, of course, difficult. We worked very hard and did not receive enough food. However, we were young. On our days off we would sit by the river, sunbathing and singing, forgetting for the moment about the world around us. We also had the company of other young men. Some people fell in love with each other; some even got married. The vows were performed by older men in the group, with even the traditional breaking of the glass. They wanted to live for today because there might not be a tomorrow.

Being brought up in a religious home, I knew that intimacy before marriage was a sin. Knowing how I felt, one of the men I was friendly with from my home town whispered in my ear, "Now all the young girls are going to God with their virginity." My answer was, "Better to give it to God." (It sounded better in Polish.)

He was caught running away, put into prison, ran away again, got caught for the second time, and was hanged in the prison in Inowroclow. After the war, I found out about this. It was very sad. He was such an intelligent person with so much life and personality in him.

One day, the order came. We were told to get our belongings together and that we would be marching out in the morning to be sent to another camp. We knew that our work in Lojewo wasn't complete.

"Why another camp?" We were all confused. Some workers ran to hide by the Polish farmers. Some of them survived. Some got caught and were either shot to death or sent back to join the others in the group.

I was approached by a friend of mine to run away with him. But because I felt obligated to protect my younger sister Hilda and brother Shymek, I refused. Later, I found out that the friend was caught and shot. He was such a smart fellow. If I would have gone with him, I would have been shot too.

One of the foremen who was in charge of the workers in Lojewo, Kozlowski, was a good Polish man. He helped some workers, men and women, get some falsified Polish identity papers. They all went into hiding and to work as Polish people. Unfortunately, one of the workers was caught and after being tortured, exposed the others. All the workers were caught. Some of them were shot, and some of the girls were sent to prison and then to Auschwitz. I met some of them there in our daily work. The stories that they told were very sad; how they were interrogated, beaten and some of the friends I had grown up with were shot.

The Gestapo arrived in the morning. We left our working camp and we were marched for hours to a large prison in Inowroclow. Many other working camps in the area were also liquidated, and the workers joined us in the prison. We were a few thousand people. It was a massive roundup of young Jewish workers who were being replaced with Polish workers. We stayed in the prison square overnight, sleeping on concrete ground.

I recall it was a beautiful night. We young people mingled with each other and conversed about where we were from and where we would be sent to work. We hoped out situation wasn't so bad.

In the morning, we got our orders to leave our belongings. First they told us to take everything with us from the working camp, and when we left the prison, they told us to leave everything. "Where you are going, you will get new things," they said. But it was always lies and deception. We were left with only the clothes that we were wearing.

From the prison, the Gestapo and the SS men, who had higher authority and were more sadistic, marched us again to a railroad station and forced us into cattle cars. The doors were closed and locked for the whole journey, leaving us in the dark. We were around

100 people to a train car and we were crowded in like cattle going to slaughter.

Each of us received a small portion of bread and the whole car got one bucket of water.

The train moved out from the station. We had no bathroom facilities, only a container for our bodily needs, and that stayed with us for the whole journey. You can imagine the conditions in the cars; the smell was horrible. Some people vomited on the floors because they could not take the foul odor. There was no room to rest. The car was so filthy. There were men, women and children in the cattle train and no privacy. We were thirsty, hungry, and tired from lack of sleep. The children were crying for food but there was none left. The conditions were unbelievable. The train was tossing us to the right and the left.

Every time the train stopped or slowed down, we all pushed ourselves toward the cracks of the wagon to see where we were for fear of the unknown. We were so confused not knowing where they were taking us.

At this time, we lost all hope.

Witkowski Family 1938

Left to Right: Haya, Shymek, Grandma Miriam Poczczywy, Bernard, my Mother Gitel, Joyce, my Father Hersh Jacob, Schlomo, Grandpa Aaron Joseph, Hilda and Hava.

Grandmother Miriam and Grandfather Berek seated in the center. My mother Gitel is top row, far left, together with her siblings

Gitel Witkowski – age 18

Hersch Jacob Witkowski – age 21
Russian Army: World War I

Joyce Witkowski – age 17

Michael Wagner – age 22

**Picture of a class at Beis Yakov, the Hebrew Girl's School
In Radziejow. (mid 1930's)**

**Boys Hebrew School. My brother Shymek is in the
center row, and is the 5th boy from the right.**

Hashoma Hatsair – Radziejow Zionist Youth Group

**Jewish Community of Radziejow 1935:
Groundbreaking for New Temple**

Engagement Photo: Joyce and Michael in 1946

Joyce Wagner Speaking to Illinois High School Class (1979)

Joyce Wagner Addresses B'nai Brith Group in Margate Florida on Yom Hashoah – the Annual Memorial observance of the Holocaust (April 2000)

Family Photo
Front Row: Hal Wagner, Sally Wagner Lipson, Joyce Wagner and
     Gilda Wagner Ross
Middle Row: Brent Wagner, Brandon Wagner, Brittany Wagner,
     Deena Lipson, Rachel Lipson
Back Grow: Michael Wagner, Michael Ross, Paul Ross, Hillary Ross,
     Eddie Ross and Brian Lipson

CHAPTER 8

AUSCHWITZ-BIRKENAU--1943

We traveled for more than two days and when it was dark, the train stopped. We heard dogs barking and saw bright lights through the cracks in the wagon. Finally, the doors opened and we were blinded by the bright lights and the strong foul stench.

Uniformed SS men and women dressed in black uniforms, shiny boots and gloves, with whips at their sides, stood with barking dogs. They shouted at us with their loud voices, "Juden raus, schnell raus!" to get out of the wagons.

Kapos with armbands (camp foremen, some of them were criminals and murderers) and other prisoners in striped clothes and shaved heads pushed us out of the wagons.

It was complete chaos.

The prisoners in striped clothes who pushed us didn't say one word! I thought they were mute, or we were in some kind of asylum. The shouting of the SS men and the Kapos was everywhere.

One of the prisoners bent over and whispered to one of us, "You are in Auschwitz, follow the rules." Others were told, if they were older they should say they were younger; but if they were younger, such as 15 years old, they should do the reverse and say they were 18 years old.

My sister Hilda was not asked her age; she was a lucky one. She was only 14 years old. The news spread quickly of our situation.

There was so much confusion. Over the entrance of the camp was a sign that read "Arbeit Macht Frei", work makes you free. We had arrived in the Auschwitz-Birkenau Concentration Camp. This was an extermination camp for mass killings. It was a huge killing factory and the last stop for thousands and thousands of Jews from Europe.

There was no escape from Auschwitz-Birkenau which was surrounded by electric wires and high watch towers filled with heavily armed members of the brutal SS-the elite unit of the German army charged by Hitler with the administration of his death factories.

They separated everyone into two groups, the men, and the women and children. Families were divided. Adults and children were crying because they didn't want to be separated from one another.

My brother Shymek, my sister Hilda and I tried desperately to stay together as much as possible. We were terrified of being separated. But in the commotion I lost sight of my brother. "Where are you Shymek? Let's stay together," I cried out. He was with the group of men. That was the last time I saw him. I was holding onto Hilda so I would not lose her too. We were ordered to march forward in a line of five.

Hilda was standing in front of me, and I told her to rub her cheeks and stand tall so she would look healthy and older. I tried to have my younger sister in front of me with the thought that whatever her destiny would be, I would follow so we would not be separated.

Ahead of us was Dr. Joseph Mengele, "the angel of death", the butcher of Auschwitz, famous for his murderous cruelty. He acted as though he was God. He pointed with his whip which way to go, to the right, or to the left, which meant who would live and who would die, who would go to work and who would be sent to the gas chambers. He was in charge, and he went through each line selecting the young and healthy workers.

We were a group of mostly young people in our twenties, still strong and healthy and able to work.

There were some children and older and sick looking people who ran out from the ghetto at the time of the liquidation who were sent to the side. They were marched straight to the gas chambers and gassed. We never saw them again.

One of my friends had her mother with her and they tore them apart to separate them. She was hysterical.

Some of the SS were even more sadistic. With force they took an infant away from its young mother's arm and threw the baby into a wagon. The mother became hysterical. She was held back only by the guns of the SS. Crying, she was forced to the women's camp of Birkenau. Some other SS assured the mother that the babies will be cared for and that they would see them later.

Always lies.

I was so relieved that my two younger sisters and parents were not with me. I cannot imagine how I would have handled our separation.

The stronger people were taken to a big building where we were showered, disinfected and all our hair was shaved off—even from our bodies. We were completely bald.

Then they took us to another room with a long table where senior prisoners sat behind the table and tattooed on our numbers.

On my left forearm, in black ink, is my number 57779 with an upside down triangle underneath, representing a Jew.

From that day on, we had no name, only our numbers.

The tattoo is so ugly, and since they put it on me, I cannot look at it. It always reminds me of the horrible place called Auschwitz and the loss of my whole family. I seldom wear a short-sleeved blouse.

The Nazis also had an identification system for prisoners. The Jews had to wear a yellow star; political prisoners, red; common criminals (Kapos), green; gypsies, brown; homosexuals, pink; and Jehovah witnesses, purple.

Naked, with our hair shaved off, we didn't recognize ourselves. I did not recognize my own sister and she did not recognize me. It was only by looking at the other women that I imagined how I looked.

We were sent to our barracks. There were men working in the camp and we walked by them without shame, because we weren't human beings anymore. We came to Auschwitz-Birkenau in cattle cars, and now, naked and bald, we felt like animals. We saw women who were skin and bones with shaved heads and striped dresses. I wondered if that was what would become of us. We never imagined that our situation could get any worse. That was when the real hell started.

The Auschwitz-Birkenau camp was called Auschwitz I, II, and III. Auschwitz I was the main official camp. Auschwitz II was the Birkenau Women's Camp and the extermination camp with the gas chambers and the crematoria. Auschwitz III was the working camp with all the factories. This was the largest Nazi death camp. There were four crematoria that were kept going constantly. When the crematoria were not able to burn all of the dead bodies, some of them were thrown into graves, sprayed with gasoline and burned.

There were six extermination or death camps: Auschwitz-Birkenau, Belzec, Chelmno, Majdanek, Sobibor and Treblinka. They were built for the sole purpose of murdering enormous numbers of Jewish people. All were named after the towns in which they operated and all were located on railroad lines for the most effective means of transporting human beings.

We were in Birkenau, in the quarantined block of the women's camp. The barracks were long buildings without a single tree or grass around them, only mud on the ground. Inside the barracks were rows of three tiered bunk beds. In the middle ran a platform of red bricks from where the Stubova and the Kapos would shout their orders.

We were given prison-striped clothing and wooden clog-type shoes. The small women got large sizes, and the tall women got smaller sizes. We were purposely given the wrong sizes to demoralize us. Even our wooden shoes were given to us in the wrong size, making it difficult to walk. We had no underwear. We were assigned to our three-tiered cojos, simple wooden frames that resembled bunk beds. We had no mattresses, no blankets and no pillows-just wooden boards with dirty straw to sleep on. Because the camp was overcrowded, 10 prisoners were assigned to each bunk bed. We slept five at the head, and five facing the other way, at the feet. We were packed in like sardines. There was hardly room to move or breathe.

We were watched by prison, "Stubovas," who were block supervisors; they were prisoners from all over Europe (Slovakian, German, and Polish girls). When somebody complained, or asked questions, they were beaten. The Stubovas would tell us that we were the lucky ones; that we came to the barracks they had to build under awful conditions.

One of the new arrivals from our transport was crying to her, "Where did they take my mother and sisters?" The Stubova grabbed her by the arm, pushed her toward the door and pointed to the crematorium and said, "You see the smoke from the chimney? There is your mother and sisters, and also fathers and brothers and the rest of your families, coming out of it!" We all started to cry hysterically. We then realized that our loved ones were killed—they were all gone, and the awful smell came from the bodies burning in the crematorium.

Our Stubova was a big, mean woman. Her words were always, "You swine" and she had a long list of other mean words. She showed you who was the boss and when she opened her mouth, you had to jump! She had a cute little room for herself which was always closed by a heavy curtain. You wouldn't dare look in there; it was like a secret place.

Every day at four in the morning we were awakened by the Stubova screaming, "Autstehen! (get up), schnell (quickly), you lazy swine!" We had to jump down from our bunk beds, and straighten up our prison dress that we slept and worked in.

Kapos, the big monsters, pushed us out of our barracks. Some of them were criminals and treated the prisoners sadistically. They assisted the SS men with their dirty work. For their brutality they got extra food and special privileges.

Quickly, we had to leave the barracks for "zahl appell," roll call, and we had to form a line of five in rain or snow, morning and night. We had to stay there shivering for hours.

I always had to make sure that my sister was next to me. The SS made us stay there in the mud to be counted till they were satisfied with the total count.

For food, we received in the morning colored water for coffee. We got some soup for lunch which was more colored water with some greens which tasted awful and smelled of rotten vegetables. In the evening we got a small portion of bread which tasted bad. This was supposed to be our daily ration. The food had some medication in it so we wouldn't have our monthly menstrual cycles. We no longer felt like women. Our periods didn't come back until some time after liberation.

We were taken to work, carrying stones in the mud to build the roads and railroad tracks to the gas chambers and crematoria. This was so the many transports of people could arrive straight to the camp crematoria rather than walking or requiring trucks to take them there.

Some days, we were forced to carry stones from one place to another just for torture. The work was exhausting but if you slowed down for a second, you were beaten, shot to death, and left in the mud of Birkenau.

One time I was carrying a very large and heavy rock and it slipped from my hands. One of the SS men noticed it and I received a beating with a rifle over my back, which I will never forget. The pain is often still there as a reminder of Birkenau. I was lucky that he didn't shoot me and leave me there in the mud. That fate was met by so many others.

The next day we were taken to do other work, digging ditches. The SS men who watched us worked us to death. We were starved and were unable to work fast enough for them. We were beaten terribly. Some were shot. We always came back to our barracks with fewer prisoners than we walked out to work with. It was extermination through work.

Some of the prisoners were taken to work the fields outside of the camp where they were able to sneak in a carrot, a potato, or a turnip. On their return from work, they were searched by the Kapos and if they found something, some of them were beaten so badly that they did not survive. The prisoners risked their own lives to bring in food for themselves or siblings. Hunger drove people to take risks.

When the SS men did not take us to work, the Stubova chased us to the outside of the quarantine barracks. In the rain and snow, we had to sit in the mud, dirty and hungry, thinking of food and disappointed that there was no grass growing in the mud. If there was, we would have had something to eat to fill our empty stomachs. Other times, we sat looking out at the chimney with smoke coming out of it. It was unreal.

We were woken during the night by the drunken voice of a German Kapo shouting, "Autstehen! (get up)." We had to jump down from our bunk beds and stay there, half asleep, and listen to her screaming and receiving beatings from her whip. When she got tired, she sent us back to our beds. Exhausted and in pain, we tried to go back to sleep to be ready in the morning for our roll call and day of hard work and more punishment.

Death and brutality were everywhere. Murder had become a daily task for the SS men.

We were hungry all the time. Sometimes, you considered yourself very lucky to find a potato peel because it tasted delicious on a piece of bread. Our conditions were unbelievable. We were filthy and had no soap or water to keep ourselves clean. We were left to delouse ourselves, to physically pick them off of our own bodies.

There was also a typhus epidemic in the camp which was spread by lice. People started dying like flies from the disease and starvation.

Not far from our barracks was the latrine block, supervised by the latrine Kapos. Inside were rows of wooden boards with holes for seats in them. The smell inside was awful. Some prisoners were so sick and if they tried to use them a little longer, they were chased out and beaten with a stick by the latrine Kapos. Some of the prisoners were so small that their feet were dangling in the air, and they had to hold on for their life, not to fall in the dirt.

My sister and I both had diarrhea either from the unsanitary conditions we lived in, or from the chemicals that were added to our soup and bread, or from the cold. The worst part was when we had to use the latrine which was about twice daily. It was almost impossible to get in there. The lines were so long and when you were finally lucky to get inside, you had to get out very quickly without completely relieving yourself for fear of being punished.

Chased out of the latrine barracks, looking around you, the scene was so shocking. There were sick people slumped on the ground in pain, unable to get up. Some were dead and left lying in the mud.

For me, not having underwear and not being able to control the diarrhea that dripped on my legs and wooden shoes was so degrading. All my life I had been a perfectionist and keeping myself clean was a way of life.

With no water to keep ourselves clean we had to use other means. In the summer, instead of drinking all of the coffee (dirty water) they gave us, I took a sip of it and used the rest to wash my face in it. In the winter, when we had snow, we washed in the snow, and then we dried ourselves with our clothes, instead of towels.

Our first months in Birkenau were very scary and emotional. I lost friends from our group to the typhus epidemic and starvation. People were dying every day, and we became surrounded by dead bodies. I went to sleep at night with a sick prisoner and woke up with a dead person next to me. Prisoners looking like skeletons were walking around us like zombies, "musselmaenner". They gave up on living. The smoke and fire were constantly visible. The stench of burning flesh was always in our nostrils and burned our eyes. It took our strength and lives away just smelling it and knowing from where it came. It came from the flesh of our Jewish people, burning in the crematoria. Our people, young and old, were wiped out and lost forever with the future generations never to be born.

We, the new arrivals, who were the lucky ones to survive the selections, envied the dead. They did not have to suffer anymore, and they did not have to anticipate what was awaiting them. Our lives had no value. We were worthless, and the SS men and the Kapos could do to us whatever pleased them—murder, torture, and cruelty was a game to them. To us, it was life or death.

By the fall of 1941, the first gassing with Zyklon B occurred in the gas chambers of Auschwitz-Birkenau. Whole trains, loaded with Jewish people, would arrive at the camp daily. Whole families together were sent to the gas chambers and then taken to the crematoria. There they were given "showers," but instead of water, the poisonous gas Zyklon B was sprayed and they were choked to death.

Fifteen thousand living humans were murdered each day.

The gold teeth of the dead were pulled out and melted down, and the gold was sent to Germany to keep the war machine going. The hair of the murdered victims was cut, and collected by the Nazis for making mattresses. Those were unprecedented acts of barbarism committed by a country that called itself, "cultured."

When we stood to be counted every day, the Stubovers and their helpers brought out the dead bodies of those prisoners who died during the night. They also had to be counted. They were piled up, as high as haystacks, one body on top of another, in front of us—a hill of dead bodies. In line, the ones who couldn't physically stand to be counted were held up by others, a little longer, when there was hardly any hope for these sick prisoners. The Kapos would pick up the severely sick and put them, still breathing, next to the dead bodies to be taken to the crematorium.

This went on day, after day, after day. It was so heartbreaking seeing the skeletons lying there dead so close to where we were standing.

I saw my two sick friends, who were sisters, alive in the evening, and the next morning, they were both dead outside the barracks, such beautiful young girls. Did they die a natural death or did they make a decision to die together instead of being taken by selection to the gas chambers. This question is always on my mind when I think about them. These young girls were from Aleksondrow. I visited them before the war in their beautiful home with loving parents and a brother. Their father was a furrier and made a good living. None of them survived.

Sitting outside our quarantined barracks, I saw transports of thousands of people coming in from all over Europe.

I witnessed women holding their infants in their arms, and small children holding on to their parents' and grandparents' hands, some dressed nicely, some poorly. Rich and poor marching straight, right past us to the gas chamber, not knowing what was about to happen to them. I will never forget those tragic scenes.

Sometimes, some of the people were given soap and towels to distract them from what was really coming. Other times, they were pushed in like cattle and when there was no more room for the children they were just thrown in, over the heads of the others to be gassed.

We knew what their fate was.

We saw the smoke coming out of the chimney of the crematoria. The stench of burning flesh was everywhere. Everyday there were selections when the SS would choose the sick prisoners or others, at random, and send them to the gas chambers.

The word among the prisoners in Auschwitz-Birkenau was, "You enter the camp by the gate and leave it through the chimney."

And we also used to say, "You see the fire and the smoke from the chimneys? That's where we will end up."

We thought the only way out of our misery was through the chimney of the crematorium. It was unbelievable for any prisoners to survive in those conditions.

At night, I would lay in my bunk bed, infested with lice, hungry, cold and cry myself to sleep. Why this inhumane treatment? Why the transports? Why this constant smoke and fire coming out of the chimney?

Why doesn't somebody try to stop it? Why? Why? And there was no answer.

I wanted to make myself useful for survival, and in my parents' store, we used to sell glass panels and I knew how to cut glass. I once approached a passing SS man and told him that I am a glazier. I told him there were broken windows in our barracks and if he would give me some glass and supplies, I could fix them. He looked at me and passed me by without saying one word. He could have taken out a gun and shot me, like they did to other prisoners, just for fun. I was just lucky.

When I think back to this incident, I wonder how naïve I was. How could I have done a thing like that? Addressing an SS man was punishable by death. Wasn't I thinking or didn't I care what would happen to me? It must have been that I was not thinking because at that time I still had my sister with me, and that always kept me going.

In Dr. Joseph Mengele's laboratory, he performed sterilizations and experiments on men, women and children—especially on pregnant women and twins. He was also experimenting on how to develop a perfect German race. We the prisoners were their guinea pigs who lived in constant danger.

The first year when I was in Birkenau, on the sacred fast day of Yom Kippur, I got my portion of soup and it was daylight. I could not make myself eat it, which would break the fast. I hid the container with the soup outside the barracks and waited till it got dark to eat my meal.

With all the tragedies that were going on around us, the prisoners were losing faith in God and questioning, "Where is God?" "Why did you desert us and allow so much misery and murdering of the Jewish people?"

In all this confusion and doubt, I still couldn't break the tradition in which I was raised. I did not lose faith in God. I would talk to God and pleaded, "God from heaven, please help us! How can you allow this cruel murdering to happen?"

Who would believe that there was an orchestra in Birkenau?

From the prisoners, the SS men selected good musicians and singers to entertain them after a long day of torturing and sending thousands of people to the gas chambers. They wanted good musicians to help them relax so that they would be able to continue their cruel acts on prisoners, day after day.

The musicians also played for the prisoners every morning and evening, when we marched to and from work, in the snow, rain and cold.

We marched past a platform where women prisoners/musicians were dressed nicely in uniforms of blue skirts and striped jackets, sitting on chairs. We envied them with their beautiful clean outfits and their shining shoes; not like us in the torn, dirty, striped dresses, wooden shoes; skinny and hardly able to walk.

The orchestra played marches for us, to march in step with the music on the way to the gates of the camp as we went to different places to work.

Some prisoners, the skeletons who could not march in step to the music and keep up with the other prisoners and SS with their dogs, were in trouble. The SS men sent their vicious dogs to attack those prisoners who were then bitten terribly to the bone, picked up, and taken straight to the crematorium.

Those dogs had vicious eyes and when they looked at you, you were so scared; you felt like they were ready to tear you apart for the smallest reason.

That was going on every day, morning and evening. It was a living nightmare.

I remember one morning when we were marched out to work and the orchestra was playing. A truck full of naked young men drove by, with their strong voices singing the Hatikvah, a Zionist anthem, on their way to the crematorium.

It was an expression of their defiance in the face of death.

Every time I hear the Hatikvah, I remember them. This image comes to my memory very often. I will never be able to forget them and I wonder, "Was my brother Shymek one of them?"

We lived in constant fear of dying and the orchestra was playing.

I witnessed the hanging of so many prisoners. The hangings were done for the smallest reasons or for no reason at all, just for the thrill of the SS; stealing a potato was a reason. Trying to escape or being suspected of belonging to a resistance group was also a reason.

The whole women's camp was ordered to the prison square where they constructed a gallows and they brought the prisoners out for the hanging. We all had to watch it. Sometimes for hours we had to watch the people hanging. We wondered, "Will this ever end?" The hangings were cruel and sadistic beyond belief.

One beautiful prisoner named Mola had a job as a translator in the office of the SS. She could not stand what was going on in the camp and wanted to let the world know what was happening in Auschwitz-Birkenau, about the mass gassing and the cruelty toward the Jewish people. She had a boyfriend, a handsome Polish man, who also had a better position in the men's camp in Auschwitz. They planned an escape and ran away.

As a result, we prisoners had to stay outside our barracks for hours for roll call to be counted. After being free for a few days, unfortunately Mola and her boyfriend were caught and brought back to Auschwitz-Birkenau and were tortured for days.

One day, the whole women's camp in Birkenau was forced to stand in the camp center square for hours where again they put up gallows. When they brought Mola out, she looked awful. She was badly beaten. One of the SS men spoke and wanted to show all of us prisoners what would happen if one of us tried to escape. When the SS men were ready to hang her, she started screaming, "Don't do that! I want to be taken to the gas chambers and be gassed, like my whole family and the other Jewish people!" She took out a razor blade that was hidden behind her ear and slit her wrist. They took her away, half dead.

The SS men did not accomplish what they intended to do. We, the prisoners who witnessed it, thought we would not be returned to our barracks alive. Mola's boyfriend was punished by hanging and the whole men's camp in Auschwitz had to witness it.

Once, I got sick with a high fever and was hallucinating that I lost my mind, and thought some people were pointing fingers at me. I started screaming that I wanted to die. My sister Hilda calmed me down and assured me that nothing was wrong with me.

We kept each other alive. I needed her to encourage me and to keep going. She needed me, too. I couldn't bear the thought of losing her. The thought of her being taken to the gas chamber was heartbreaking for me.

We struggled to survive together. I had to remain alive to take care of her as long as I could. We always wanted to give each other an extra bite of our own bread, but we both refused.

I had to be strong for her and protect her, like a parent. The thought of living longer than her was unthinkable. When she got sick with a cold and fever, I dragged her out to roll call. I always pushed her to go to work, and not stay behind in the barracks. We thought that as long as you worked, you had a better chance of survival. But when you stayed behind in the barracks, you took a big chance on being sent to the so-called hospital or gas chambers by the SS men or the Kapos. As for myself, I was skin and bones, and my life was in danger every day of being taken away in a selection to the gas chambers. My sister looked much stronger than me and her hair was growing back. She was a pretty girl.

My sister Hilda had a beautiful voice, and even in our misery in Birkenau, I recall when she was sitting on our bunk bed and singing with another girl. This other young girl, Jenny, became a professional singer. If my sister had survived, maybe her future would have been as a singer too.

I think of all those young innocent children going to the gas chambers and the other children who were so sadistically killed by the SS men—we heard about living children being burned in the pits because the gas chambers were too full.

Jewish children were not permitted to live under the Nazi regime.

I wonder how could any human being hurt or murder an innocent child? What has our world lost by the death of one and a half million children? How many were destined to be the next Einstein, Barbara Streisand, Leonard Bernstein, or Stephen Spielberg?? I think about the accomplishments of these thousands of children who were never given the chance to see where life would take them. I think about all that they could have given back to society. They could have grown up to be professors, scientists, researchers, doctors and entertainers.

One day, I remember very clearly sitting outside our quarantined barracks with some other girls. It was a nice, clear, sunny day and far away, we could see the Carpathian mountains. Looking out at the world beyond the electric wires of Birkenau, we were talking about how beautiful the world was. There was a living world outside this hell and we were all facing death and the crematorium.

We were talking about what lay ahead for us. Is this the last day of our lives? First our dignity was taken away, then we were robbed of our possessions and when nothing was left, they were taking our lives away. We girls made a promise to each other that if by some miracle one of us would survive, we would tell the world what happened in this hell called Auschwitz-Birkenau.

This book is my "promise kept" to them.

And when I speak to high school students, I tell them this talk is a result of the promise we girls made that day, and it is my promise kept to those young girls who did not survive. In my memory, I see their faces and remember the words, "Please God, let one of us survive."

Some of the girls were working in the warehouse where they collected the looted possessions from the people who arrived in Auschwitz-Birkenau from all over Europe. They called it the Canada warehouses, the rich warehouses. Two thousand women prisoners worked there. Some of the people who arrived in Auschwitz-Birkenau had luggage. The rich carried suitcases with fortunes in them because they were told that they were going to be resettled in other places; and they brought all their valuable possessions to Auschwitz-Birkenau.

The jewelry, gold and other valuables were sent to the Third Reich's main banks, "Deutsche Reichsbank", to help the German war efforts. The clothes and other personal items were also sent to Germany. The perishable food was given to the SS and elite, influential prisoners.

Some of the food and clothes were taken from the Canada warehouse by some prisoner workers for their siblings and friends. When they were caught stealing, they were severely punished.

Even in Auschwitz-Birkenau, there were two classes of prisoners, those who had, and those who had nothing.

Those who had power, the Kapos, Stubovas, some Canada workers, some kitchen workers, and others, who had privileged jobs, were able to meet with men from the men's camp. Even in this miserable place that was Auschwitz-Birkenau, dates were going on between privileged men and women—and the women were getting extra gifts and treats from the men. I am not talking about money. In my confinement there, I did not see or hear of money being exchanged between prisoners. It was always a piece of bread for a cigarette, or an onion, or other personal things.

One of the girls I knew worked in the Canada warehouse. She got acquainted with a German prisoner who was sent to Auschwitz for a crime he committed and he became a Kapo there. She had a boyfriend who was in the men's part of Auschwitz. She told the Kapo in charge there that this boyfriend was her brother, and the Kapo helped him out, and luckily her boyfriend survived.

After working in all kinds of outdoor jobs, in snow, rain and heat, and starving and being beaten, we didn't look the same.

We girls who came to Birkenau a picture of health, after a few months, we all looked like skeletons. As time went on, some were killed and others died, and all the time, others were being taken by selections to the gas chambers.

When we were given a small piece of margarine, I had a bad feeling about it. I was afraid a selection would quickly follow as it often did. As much as I looked forward to the extra little food, I was scared for the selections that would follow—to be chosen, to live or to die. We prisoners were so scared of the gas chambers that we begged to be shot instead of being taken by a selection to be gassed. Nothing seemed real to us anymore.

Why this intolerable waiting for death?

So many times when it was raining, going and coming back from our daily work, we were soaked from rain and dragging our feet in the mud. We had to stand for the role call until the count of the prisoners was correct. We were given our bread. Then, soaking wet we laid on the straw in our bunk beds until we fell asleep. When we woke-up in the morning our clothes were still wet on our bodies.

That was a typical day in Birkenau. How we survived such atrocities is unbelievable.

Being locked up in Birkenau almost a year, we were living around the crematoria with the smoke, fire, and mud on the ground, with no grass, no trees, and no birds singing. As a country girl, I grew up with nature all around me. Here in Birkenau it felt like another world where only torture, misery and death existed.

After awhile, my sister and I were lucky to be assigned an indoor job, in the Krupp ammunition factory, "Union Werke." We girls who worked there were envied by other prisoners for working indoors instead of outdoors in the mud, rain and snow. We worked there with some male prisoners from Auschwitz. Every time I got to work, I would search the group for signs of my brother Shymek hoping to catch a glimpse of him. But unfortunately I never saw him. Was he even still alive?

It was a big factory with all different kinds of machines, big and small. Where I worked, there was a long row of machines where we prisoners produced various parts.

I was assigned to a machine where I sharpened the points on nails. We were forced to provide a few boxes of finished material every day, which was impossible. We made a pact with the male prisoners who were working in the factory warehouse to give us double credit for our work. We had to cheat about our production to survive.

We took a big chance. If we were caught, we would all be shot to death.

The work went on day and night. We were supervised by German foremen and watched by the SS men and women and Kapos.

While in the factory, my sister Hilda didn't have to work so hard. She was befriended by a German woman, a Kapo prisoner, who was sent to Birkenau for refusing to divorce her Jewish husband. The German woman was assigned to watch the Jewish workers in the factory. My sister took care of her personal chores, like washing her clothes and cleaning her private quarters. She gave my sister some of the food she received from her family in Germany.

She sympathized with the Jewish prisoners. Sometimes, she looked the other way when we tried to rest for a minute at our machines. She was a good person and felt sorry for us, but still had to do her work and carry out the orders.

We missed her when she got sick. She caught typhus and died in Birkenau. She was replaced with another German Kapo who was a very mean and sadistic person and worked us very hard. Conditions deteriorated when this new Kapo assumed power over us.

Everyday after work in the Union factory, we were taken to a bathhouse where we were showered because we were working with private German foremen. They wanted to keep us clean so we wouldn't bring the dirty conditions of the camp to the factory.

Hot water to shower!

I didn't experience this for almost a year. It felt like drops from heaven. The hot water was soothing our bony bodies but often came with the threat of another selection. One time we were given soap to clean our bodies. One of the prisoners remarked, "You are cleaning yourselves with the fat of your families." Even in the little pleasures of a shower came the sad reminder of the crematorium and the loss of our loved ones.

We were often deloused. One day, our hair was checked for lice. We tried to keep our heads clean to keep the lice away from us. First they checked my sister's hair and they found it clean. When the Kapo came to check my hair, I said to her, "I keep my hair clean." She looked at me sadistically and without even checking, just to spite me, she went quickly and shaved my whole head and called me, "You Polska swinia (swine)." I was hysterical. Since my hair grew back a little, I had looked more human.

To comfort me, my sister said, "Don't cry. If your head will survive, your hair will grow back." She was so right. I will forever remember her remarks.

Very often in the bathhouse we were visited by SS men, supposedly doctors, who made selections. We had to parade naked in front of them. Those who had swollen ankles and didn't look good to them were taken to the side and sent to their deaths.

Next to my machine at the factory, there was a beautiful young girl working from Lodz. She showed me her swollen legs; she was scared of the next selection. The same day after work, we were taken again to the bathhouse and had a selection by a SS doctor. I saw when she was pulled to the side with the other sick girls. I didn't see her at her machine the next day. Instead, I saw a stronger worker, a new arrival to Birkenau.

There were machines that needed special operators. When those operators became overworked, and couldn't work any longer, they were forced to teach new, stronger arrivals their job. They used to say, "I am teaching you today, and tomorrow I will be burning in the crematorium and you will take my place." They also said, "I die today and you die tomorrow." Our lives had no meaning to the SS. Very often I prayed for miracles to keep my sister and me alive. That was the only way you could survive in the hell of Birkenau.

My sister was once selected not to come back to work the next morning. She didn't look good to the doctor/SS man. I pleaded with a Kapo not to take her away. I knew I wouldn't see her again. I did manage to save her life that time though she could have just sent me too. We were very lucky.

At another selection, my sister was selected again not to come back to work. This time I pleaded with the Stubova to save her life. In the meantime, someone else died in our barracks and we were able to replace her for my sister. As long as the count of the prisoners was correct, the Stubova didn't care. Without our hair, and being skin and bones like skeletons, we all looked alike.

After working in the Union factory for awhile, surviving all the selections, Hilda's health started to deteriorate. She could not go to work, and she could not stand to be counted in the morning. Before I left for work I kissed my sister's burning forehead from the high fever. That was the last time I saw my sister alive.

All day at my machine, I worried about her and as I had feared, after returning from work, I found her gone from the barracks.

She was not allowed to stay in the barracks and she was taken to the "revier," the so-called hospital. She was fighting to go on but her condition got worse and there was no medication to keep her alive. Having come this far, her luck ran out. She had caught typhus.

I was not allowed to go see her. Our Stubova saw her and my sister begged her to tell me that she would love to have an onion. Some of the German women prisoners were allowed to get packages from their families. I pleaded with one for an onion in exchange for my portion of bread—which was supposed to keep me alive for the day. I sent the onion to my sister.

Despite being exhausted from my long day's work in the Union factory day after day, I stood outside the hospital with hopes of being able to get in to see her alive, but could not.

One day, I was lucky to get into the hospital. It was a very big room with beds crowded close to each other. It was very noisy with sick prisoners screaming and crying for help.

Here prisoners were kept without medical care until their death, or until they were taken alive to the gas chambers. Some of them were given poisonous injections to speed the killing.

I walked around in this big room looking for my sister hoping to find her alive and calling her name, "Hilda." Then I heard a weak voice call, "here, here." I walked to the woman's bed and in it was a mere skeleton and next to her I saw an empty bed with an onion on a little shelf above it. I asked her, "Where is my sister?" She said, "Oh, she died so peacefully in her sleep." She must have been so sick that she didn't care for the onion any longer. I just left it there.

When I found out that my sister had died, it was a terrible loss but I felt I was in the same situation. I could not expect myself to survive and then, it was easier to accept her death.

Our thoughts were not on living but on death. We got used to death, it was all around us. So often I envied the dead; they did not have to suffer any longer.

Today, when I remember Hilda and think back on her death, I cry about it, but at that time in Birkenau, in the moment of sadness, I did not cry. I was relieved for her that she died peacefully in her sleep, instead of being taken alive to the gas chamber.

She was only 15 years old.

I missed my sister so much. I was left all alone. The bunk bed felt so empty. I missed having her at my side as we always tried to stay together and not be separated. I always had my sister in front of me, or next to me. I always tried to protect her.

In all the misery which we lived in, she was the cheerful one who had kept me going.

Instead of crying when my sister died, I prayed to God to take me peacefully, in the same way, in my sleep. In Birkenau, it was a blessing to die in your sleep. Then you didn't have to suffer any longer because nobody in their right mind ever hoped to get out of Auschwitz-Birkenau alive. We knew we had a death sentence on our heads. But, we were hoping to survive another day and another day.

We were young and we wanted to survive. No matter how horrible our conditions were, or how miserable I was, the will to survive was strong in me. It was unbelievable how one's mind worked in Birkenau. One minute I was ready to give up and the next minute I pinched my cheek to look healthy and was happy that I survived another selection.

The will to live was always powerful in me. I remember one incident when I was 8 years old. My mother gave me 10 grochy (cents) to buy some vegetables for soup. On the way to the store, I held the coin close to my mouth and kept repeating "onions, parsley, carrots", until I swallowed the small coin by accident. I ran home scared and crying, "Mommy, I don't want to die. I want to live."

Then I got sick. I was burning from a high-fever and was unable to go to work or stand in the morning to be counted. I was in danger if I stayed behind in the barracks. I was so afraid of being taken to the gas chambers.

"Whoever stops working, dies." That was the motto of Auschwitz-Birkenau.

Where to turn for help? Getting medication was impossible. I did not have extra bread to trade for medicine to break the high fever. Being in Birkenau for a year, I lost lots of friends from Lojewo—they were mostly all gone. I was left alone.

I was scared but I had no choice and stayed in the barracks; so they took me to the "hospital."

When we arrived there, we had to take off all our clothes. We were all naked in this large room. By a miracle, I overheard that the Stubova from our barracks was looking for one particular sick, young girl to get her out of there because all the sick prisoners from this room were being taken straight to the gas chambers regardless of their condition.

When I luckily overheard that, I got so scared and started looking for a way to sneak out of there. I felt the presence of someone pushing me out of there. I noticed a dead woman lying on the floor with her coat on; she didn't need it anymore. I took the coat off of her body and it was covered with lice. I put it on and snuck out of the hospital.

I ran to my barracks, and when I got there, the Stubova wanted me to go back to the hospital. She said, "They have your number there. What am I going to do with you here? Do you think that I am going to die for you?" I told her, "Kill me here. Let them shoot me here. You are not going to get me back to the hospital to go to the gas chamber alive." That's how scared I was of the gas chambers and the crematorium—I did not want to end up in the furnace.

Luckily, she did not send me back—for the moment, she actually acted more like a human being. Some Kapos and Stubovas did feel sorry for us sometimes and did act more humanely toward the prisoners.

At about the same time, another woman passed away in our barracks and they took her dead body to the hospital in my place. People were dying there all the time. I cheated death again and I inherited a coat from a dead body and striped prison clothes from another dead body and I was still alive.

The next day, I was back at work, healthy, at my machine. Fear gave me back my strength.

I did not contact typhus in Birkenau because I had typhus before the war when there was an epidemic in our town. At that time, I lost my oldest brother Meyer and lots of school friends. Supposedly, having had typhus, I was immune to the disease for the next nine years.

One day we got up in the morning for the roll call, and we saw across from our barracks behind the wires, whole families, men, women and children living together. We found out the people were from Theresienstadt, the ghetto-camp in Czechoslovakia. After a few months, in the middle of 1944, we noticed the barracks were empty. They were all gone. Rumors spread that the people were sent to the gas chambers.

There was also a gypsy camp where the gypsies lived together; we could often hear their music. One day, there was no sound from the camp. It was empty. They were all taken to the gas chambers to be killed.

When Hitler came to power, he and his followers were against Jews, gypsies, Jehovah's Witnesses, homosexuals, and people who were against his policies. He also sought to eliminate mentally retarded and disabled German people. When a German baby was born disabled, instead of giving the child medical attention, it was given a lethal injection. Older disabled children and adults were removed from hospitals and put to death.

Hitler's Nazi regime had the mission of total extermination of all Jews. According to Hitler's orders, all of the Jewish people had a death sentence on our heads and not one European Jew should remain alive.

We were not meant to survive with our numbers on our arms to show the world the real truth of what happened in his concentration camps, to bear witness to his cruelty.

We survivors have the responsibility never to let the world forget.

The Nazi party with their propaganda accomplished the highest degree of antisemitism that had ever existed. There were many who collaborated with the Nazis and stood by and let the Holocaust happen. But there were also some good people like Raoul Wallenberg, the Swedish diplomat, the Danish people and others, who saved Jewish lives because they had empathy for others.

There were groups of anti-Nazi resistance in Germany, and a group of Nazis who did not approve of the way Hitler was running Germany; the latter group of German officers tried to assassinate Hitler. In July of 1944, a bomb exploded in a room where Hitler met with his highest officers. But unfortunately, their plan failed. The news spread quickly in Auschwitz-Birkenau and we prisoners who heard it were devastated. We were hoping that something like that would happen and our misery would be over; and thousands and thousands of Jewish people could still be saved. But it was not meant to be.

After the attempt on Hitler's life, Hitler and his followers went on a campaign of more inhumane treatment and extermination of Jewish people. Transports from Europe arrived with greater speed.

The Allied forces were gradually winning back some of the territories that Germany had conquered. Hitler's forces were being pushed back on three fronts: from the Italy invasion from the south, from the Normandy France invasion in the north, and from the Russians on the west.

The Germans were losing the war and we Jewish people were still paying with our lives.

In March of 1944, Germany occupied Hungary and soon after, many transports arrived in Auschwitz-Birkenau from Hungary. Most of the Jewish people were brought to the main killing center which was Auschwitz-Birkenau. The Nazis were committed to exterminating all Jews, their final solution to be Juden-frei (free of Jews). The gas chambers and the ovens were working constantly around the clock, day and night. Jewish people were gassed there and burned. Their bodies turned to ashes. The Canada warehouse was overcrowded with the high amount of baggage that arrived with the transports.

At that time, we had "Blocksperre," the doors of the barracks were closed. We were not allowed to go out or look out of the doors. We were all confined to our barracks for hours. Supposedly, the SS men didn't want us to see what was going on. They didn't want witnesses to their crimes and mass murders. They were bringing people to the gas chambers. Most of the new arrivals were sent right to their deaths.

Sometimes, there were selections when the SS men picked out some young people to replace those Jewish workers who had become walking skeletons, only skin and bones, who could not work any longer. The new arrivals were much stronger than those of us who had been in Birkenau for more than a year or two.

At that time the camp was especially overcrowded. The SS men had to make room for the new arrivals replacing the other sick prisoners. "Blocksperre," was in effect for a few hours everyday.

Some times when we had a "Blocksperre," the SS men would spontaneously pick any barracks for a selection. They would pick out the sick and skeleton-like people and send them straight to the gas chambers. Or, for more sadistic torture, some of the prisoners were sent to another barrack, where they kept them naked and without food or water for days, starved them to death, and then sent them to the gas chambers.

The SS men often came up with new brutalities. Their cruelty had no limits.

Some of the SS men would knock the prisoners down to the ground, and then with their foot on the prisoner's throat, they would choke them to death.

At other times after a selection, they would let some prisoners whose numbers were written down go back to the barracks with the lucky ones who were spared this time from selection. These unfortunate prisoners had to sit and wait for their deaths. The next day, their numbers were called and they were taken away to the gas chambers. We never saw them again. That was our life in Birkenau. If you were lucky enough to live longer, you were losing old friends who were sometimes replaced by new arrivals.

We always questioned, "How could this happen in a civilized world?" "Where is humanity, to be silent to these atrocities?"

"Why didn't the leaders of the Allied Forces bomb the railroad tracks leading to Auschwitz?" When I was working in the ammunition factory, a few times we heard the bombs falling not too far from our working place. Each falling bomb gave us hope of survival even though our lives were in danger. We were hoping the bombs would fall on the railroad tracks leading to Auschwitz; so many Jewish people could have been saved.

One day after work, instead of marching us back to our old barracks we were transferred to other separate barracks in Auschwitz. As I recall we were given beautiful silk nightgowns to sleep in. Our thoughts went back to the Jewish women who slept in these clothes before; who lived in their beautiful homes, in luxury, with their families. They must have come from Paris or other big cities in Europe. What happened to these women? Were they given the rough prison clothes and sent to hard work and starvation? Or were they sent straight to the gas chambers?

Life in the new barracks was much cleaner. We were taken to showers every day. Our food rations were the same as before. The Kapos and the Foremen worked us to death. Hard work and life in the camps took its toll on me. I became very weak.

Every day at Birkenau, I saw dead bodies lying next to the electric wires. Skin and bones, they took their own lives because they couldn't handle any longer the hunger, dysentery, and typhus. They chose the electric wires instead of being taken to the gas chambers.

I was also skin and bones walking around like a zombie. I had no strength left in me and I was ready for a selection and the gas chamber. I stopped caring what would happen to me. Life had no meaning to me anymore. How much misery can one person endure? My sister Hilda was gone. I was left all alone and I too wanted to end my life by touching the electric wires that surrounded the whole camp. I could not fight any longer and I was ready to accept my death.

I walked over to the wires and reached out my arm ready to touch it with my finger, but I could not do it. Something pushed me back. In front of me, I had visions of my father reminding me what he had taught us children: God gives life and he is the only one who can take it away. I never forgot that and I could not do it.

I walked away from the fence with hope, not ready to give up yet. I was determined to live.

I call this another one of my many miracles and another one of the reasons why I survived.

To survive you also had to have a purpose in life. In the beginning, my purpose in living was my sister Hilda. When she was gone, I held on to the hope that someone from my family would survive and return home. I wanted to be there for them.

In Birkenau we prisoners had to have faith in God and ourselves not to give-up, and had to have strength to go on living. You also had to be lucky not to be taken by selection, shot, beaten to death, or to get sick. With lots of luck and faith, some of us were able to live through the miserable conditions of Birkenau and had a better chance of survival.

Every six months, the SS men selected a group of male prisoners to work in the gas chambers and crematoria. They were called the Sonderkommandos. They were forced to do the work and carry out the orders to the victims who were sent to the gas chambers. They had to pull the gold teeth out of the dead bodies, cut their hair, and remove their gold jewelry before they put them into the crematorium. It was a heartbreaking job. Some of them recognized the bodies of their families and children. Many committed suicide and many were held back by others, with the hopes of getting revenge. After six months, they were then sent to the gas chambers and replaced by other prisoners; they were silenced by their deaths. The SS men did not want witnesses to their crimes and mass murders.

By late 1944, a group of Sonderkommandos knew that their time was up and that they too, would soon be cremated. They knew that the world was silent, that nobody cared about us, even after the underground was sending out messengers to tell the world what was happening in Auschwitz-Birkenau. Prisoners from the Resistance got some radios from the Canada warehouse and they listened to the newscasts to bolster the morale of the prisoners. The news spread quickly from mouth to mouth that the Germans were losing the war. Yet, in Birkenau, crematoria were still working day and night.

The Resistance was planning a revolt, a general uprising, which they were afraid might be too risky. Instead, the Sonderkommandos decided to blow up the gas chamber and the crematoria themselves. They got in touch with the women prisoners who worked in the explosive section in the Union ammunition factory where I was also working in another section. A few of the girls who had access to the explosives were able to smuggle out some explosives to make a bomb.

The plan worked, and on October 7, 1944, the Sonderkommandos blew up crematorium #3 and killed some Kapos and SS men. They all ran out from behind the electric wires, but unfortunately, they were caught and shot.

After all their planning, they did not survive.

There was a lot of commotion going around at the Union factory that day. From far away, we could see the thick smoke coming from the side of the crematorium. Rumors spread quickly that one of the crematoria was bombed. It was a very happy day for all of us because we were able to stop the killing of five thousand people a day. It was also a scary day. There were more SS men than usual inside the factory. We were afraid the SS would take revenge for the killing of some of their men and punish us with more starvation, shootings, and hangings, or send us all from the factory to the gas chambers.

Then, one day after work, we were not allowed to go back to the barracks. Instead we were marched to the execution grounds to witness an execution. We were surrounded by many SS men and their dogs. They had set up gallows, and the SS men brought out four heroic, battered, young girls who had bravely smuggled out the dynamite explosives for blowing up the crematorium. The four girls were executed by hanging in front of our own eyes. A few days before the hanging, one of them who was considered the leader, Roza Robota, sent out a message in Hebrew, "Hasak Hamatz"—be strong and brave.

I stood there and witnessed these hangings and will never forget it. It was heartbreaking; such a tragedy, so close to liberation.

One month after the revolt, in November of 1944 the SS stopped the gassing of people in Auschwitz.

By January of 1945, the Germans were losing the war. We heard bombs being dropped not far away from Auschwitz. We knew that the liberation was close at hand. We, the prisoners, still had no hope of survival.

With the approach of the Russian army, the frightened SS men began burning and destroying the camp records. They also blew up the crematoria to conceal the evidence of their heinous crimes. They sent out to Germany some of the valuable possessions from the Canada warehouse that they had accumulated from the Jewish people.

They did not know how to do away with the prisoners with so little time. They planned to send us to other death camps to be killed, but they didn't have trains available for the transport of the prisoners anymore. The only choice they had was to march us "musselmaenner" out of Auschwitz-Birkenau.

When the Russian Army reached Auschwitz-Birkenau on January 27, 1945, the gates of the concentration camp were opened to expose the barbaric conduct of Nazi Germany. The Russians were shocked at the unbelievable scenes of brutality, starvation, and mass killing. No one could imagine such atrocities. There were five thousand sick people left there because the Nazis did not have time to kill them all off. After a few days some of them died.

The SS were not able to empty the Canada warehouses, so a great deal of stolen merchandise was left behind. The Russians also found the human hair, shoes and other items left from the dead people.

That was Auschwitz-Birkenau where over one million Jewish people were murdered and I spent almost two years of my life in a living nightmare so close to death.

I still do not know how I survived. What my eyes witnessed there cannot fully be expressed in words. Often I can see it all so clearly, like it happened just yesterday.

But the liberation of the camp was not the end of my suffering.

CHAPTER 9

THE DEATH MARCH--JANUARY 1945

As the Russian liberators of the camps drew nearer, the SS became increasingly frantic. There just was not time to kill all of us. So we were assembled for one last role call, and then they marched 60,000 of us out of Auschwitz-Birkenau.

Today this event is referred to as the Death March.

It was January 1945 and snow was falling. It was a beautiful white world, but for us prisoners it meant walking in the cold and wet. Snow turned to slippery ice, which made the going extremely difficult. We were forced to march in the snow and sub-zero temperatures all the way from Poland to Germany!

Thousands collapsed when they could not walk any further. And at the end of the massive column of prisoners came the SS Stormtroopers with their vicious dogs. Prisoners were shot and thrown into ditches along the road.

The SS had orders from their superiors that all Jews were to be killed. Their goal was to insure that no prisoner would be left alive to be liberated by the advancing Russian Army.

We stopped for one night to rest in a large farm along the road. Some of us were fortunate and were able to rest inside of a barn. Many prisoners were simply too sick and weak to force themselves into the barn. They were left sitting outside in the snow and freezing weather, huddled together, to try to keep warm. In the morning many were found frozen to death. I considered hiding in the barn to escape from the continuation of the march, but ultimately I decided against this idea. I was scared that I would be caught and shot.

I had no energy left in me, and still I forced myself to continue to walk, mile after mile—dragging my feet, my body frozen and hungry. But I was falling behind the main group. I looked around and there was not a single familiar face. There was no one from the Union factory; no one from my barracks. I was left behind. I was walking with a group of strangers who were half dead walking skeletons. I thought: "Why am I forcing myself to walk? For what?" We would all be killed anyway.

Slowly I caught up with the others who were the stronger of the marchers. Now my mind had become concentrated upon one thing: to keep marching and to stay alive. The will to live was still strong in me—even in this new misery called the Death March. The snow, cold and wind were blowing at my hairless head and face. My wooden shoes were covered with heavy, wet snow which made walking even harder. I pushed myself forward so as not to fall behind again because I knew it meant death by a bullet from the SS guard.

I wanted to live, to keep the promise that we girls had made to each other. We had pledged to survive to tell the world of the hellish horrors we had endured during the Hitler Nazi regime. I witnessed the horror, starvation, exhaustion, torturing, shooting, hanging and beating of the prisoners to death. It is impossible to truly describe this.

Some prisoners who could not continue the march were helped by family, friends or others and pushed forward a little longer. When somebody wanted to give up, to sit down in the snow begging, "Just let me sleep," we knew we were about to lose another prisoner to an SS bullet.

It is hard to describe the situation that we were in. The genocide of the "final solution" was continuing on that march. Murder was continuing by starvation, freezing weather conditions, and the guns and dogs of the SS. The scene was beyond belief.

Every morning as we rose to continue our walk we wondered: "Would we survive another day?" Gunshots rang out with increasing frequency as more and more prisoners met their death at the hands of the SS.

One shot/one death. And the rest of us skeletons marched on without any food, and the frozen conditions we endured. Sometimes, I compare myself to the soldiers in a battle in the war. Two soldiers are in the trenches. Enemy bullets are flying toward them. One gets shot by a bullet and dies. The other, the lucky one, continues fighting and survives. That was me, one of the lucky ones, destined to survive.

After walking for almost three days we were separated into groups. Those who could still walk were put into open train cars. There was snow up to our knees. The SS packed us together very tightly but this time we didn't mind. The closeness of our bodies kept us a little warmer in the freezing January weather. Then the train began to move, and the wind and snow whipped over us as we stood in the open cars.

We wondered if we would survive the journey, and had no idea what our final destination was intended to be. Whenever we passed a building with a tall chimney, I thought this was our final destination where we would be killed by gassing.

When we passed a forest clearing I would think this is where we will all be unloaded and shot. But the train continued on.

Still, to the last minute, I did not trust the SS men.

The daylight turned to darkness when we finally came to another camp.

CHAPTER 10

RAVENSBRUECK

Ultimately the train took our group to yet another death/working camp called Ravensbrueck. Established in May, 1935, this was the only major women's concentration camp. Located in the north of Germany, it was situated in a hidden location with access to good roads. Like all other concentration camps, prisoners at Ravensbrueck suffered death by weakness, starvation, hanging, shooting and beating on a daily basis. Over 92,000 people were murdered there, many of them children.

When we arrived there the camp was already filled to capacity. So we newcomers were left in an open tent that had been pitched on ground covered with snow with some straw on top of it. The tent provided very little in the way of shelter, and snow blew in on us from all sides. It was freezing cold.

When I removed my wooden shoes, I noted that one of my feet was swollen from frostbite—the result of prolonged exposure to cold and snow. I started limping, and found that I could not put the shoe back on my swollen foot. Some of the girls found a blanket and others got some sewing supplies and together we sewed a pair of slippers which I then wore in the snow. We tried to help each other as best we could.

Conditions were unbelievably bad, and we were treated inhumanely. Food was the occasional piece of bread and watery "soup"—never anything warm.

I was skin and bones and could only walk with great difficulty.

After a period of days it was announced that those who could still walk would be transferred to yet another working camp. There would be another selection from our group that had come from Birkenau.

I could not walk straight and was limping badly. I prayed to God that I would pass the selection. I wanted desperately to get out of Ravensbrueck. Having come this far, I wanted to survive.

When my turn came for the selection I was ordered to walk twenty steps forward. I stepped out, and to my own amazement I walked by the female SS officer perfectly. I had no limp!

Somehow, I felt like I was holding onto my sister Hilda's arm for support. We had always helped each other and here again, she was by my side encouraging me, "You can do it, just walk straight like you encouraged me at the selection on our arrival to Auschwitz-Birkenau." It was unbelievable; it was another one of my miracles.

CHAPTER 11

MECKLENBURG

This time for our transfer we were loaded onto buses. My thoughts turned again to the buses that took the Jews of Radziejow to Chelmno, where they were gassed. After traveling for hours we arrived late at night at the working camp of Mecklenburg.

This was a small camp located close to an airfield. Our living quarters had once housed German pilots. These accommodations were much nicer—far superior to the filthy barracks of Birkenau. We still had bunk beds but now, instead of dirty straw, we had mattresses with pillows and blankets. We finally had enough water to keep ourselves clean.

Our working conditions were better as well. When we went out to work, we were supervised by old German soldiers with guns instead of SS Stormtroopers and their dogs.

There were still a few of the SS, and they watched us while we worked.

Our food rations were still small.

We were cleaning the airfield of debris from the Allied air raids. We also dug underground shelters and ditches.

Often at night our barracks shook from the nearby bombings. In the mornings when we would emerge from the barracks fires would be burning all around us. The airfield was a testing site for the Luftwaffe—the German Air Force. It must have been a strategic base to have attracted so much Allied attention.

Life in Mecklenburg was a little easier but our lives were still in danger from the bombings so close to our barracks. There were no bunkers for the prisoners. We felt that the liberation was not too far away and the question was always on our minds, "After so much suffering, will we survive Mecklenburg?"

With my swollen legs and my limp I could not walk out with the other girls to work. My feet just could not carry my body any longer. I begged one of the SS men to let me work inside of the camp. I explained, as l had tried to do once before at Birkenau, that I had glazier skills and could fix windows that were being shattered in the air raids. Amazingly, this time I was lucky and he agreed. He assigned another girl and me to work in the warehouse. There were lots of tools, but unfortunately no glass to repair the windows. So instead we worked there for several weeks cleaning up the warehouse.

When the work was completed we were assigned to a different building where we collected the dirty clothes from the SS and German soldiers, and exchanged them for clean ones. The two of us also retrieved food for the soldiers and the SS. We had to push a small wagon that normally would be drawn by a horse. Under the watchful eyes of our SS supervisor, we became the horses as we took the cart to a nearby city.

I was in pain, but it was worth the effort because when we reached the food-supply warehouse the German woman who was in charge felt sorry for the two of us. We were skinny undernourished Jewish prisoners. She secretly gave us some bread and liverwurst. It felt like a blessing from heaven.

Several times on the return trip we had to stop because of Allied bombings all around the city. We would exit the road and hide with the SS in a ditch. When the bombings would stop we would climb out of the ditch and survey a landscape of white fields and nearby burning buildings.

We knew that our liberation was near. The SS man was not happy that we were witnesses to these events. What an unlikely trio: two Jewish concentration camp inmates and one frightened member of the arrogant SS hiding together in the same ditch. At that moment we were all equals, and equally scared to death of the bombs dropping from the sky so close to us.

At another time, we were in the food warehouse when the air-raid sirens sounded and the townspeople began running to the nearby woods. The SS trooper who was watching over us, then abandoned us and ran for cover as well in order to save his own life.

The two of us prisoners were left alone, and we followed the crowds to the woods. We were wearing normal street clothes that we had been given in Mecklenburg, not our standard striped prison garb. With our hair now beginning to grow out a little bit, we looked more human. We also felt a little better thanks to that German woman from the warehouse who had provided us with a little bit of additional food.

At that time we could have run away but the Germans were still in power and there was no place to hide. It felt like all doors were still closed to us and if we were caught, we would be shot. We knew at the camp there was a bed to sleep in and hope of survival. So when the air-raid was over we went back to the warehouse looking for the SS trooper who was in charge of us.

Looking back, it was ironic that we prisoners were now looking for our captor to take us back to the work camp.

So we returned again to the camp, under the watchful eyes of our SS supervisor. My girl friend and I looked at each other, wondering if we had done the right thing.

After a period of working together this girl and I separated. I never saw that young woman again. Sometimes I think about her. She was such a gentle, refined person. I wonder: did she survive? I think about other girls with whom I shared a bunk bed at Mecklenburg. One was younger than me. When there were air raids at night this girl would give out terrified screams. Ultimately she became ill and was taken to the hospital. She was left behind, so close to liberation.

We were in Mecklenburg for a few months, and again, the Russians were not too far from us.

One morning the SS and some of the old soldiers again marched us out of the work camp. Those who could not walk, as well as all of the sick prisoners from the hospital were thrown into ditches, sprayed with gasoline, and burned. We saw the flames coming from the woods near our working camp, and it was a tragic and sad scene. We knew we had lost more of our friends who would not survive to see the day of liberation.

As we marched out of the camp we found ourselves accompanied by German refugees. They walked alongside of us, their wagons filled with belongings, food and cans of milk. They were fleeing the approaching Russian army.

The Germans were justified in their fear of the Russians, who were taking terrible revenge as they pushed ever deeper into German territory. The Russians had lost 20 million people to the German invasion of their homeland. Russian soldiers were also ever mindful of the awful treatment that Russian prisoners of war had received at the hands of the German Army, and of the SS men who had abused Russian soldiers badly at Auschwitz. Many Russian POW's had been sent to their deaths in the Auschwitz gas chambers, in direct violation of the rules of the Geneva Convention.

We saw the German Army in retreat, but we were still under the watchful eyes of the SS. That did not last for long. We watched as the SS cowards removed their uniforms, put on civilian clothes, and then ran to save their own lives. The old German soldiers were left in charge. If one of us tried to run away they would shout, "We will shoot you if you try to escape."

Liberation was so very close now, and yet we were still not certain that we would survive to see it happen.

The German soldiers who were guarding us marched us farther away from the approaching Russian army. Again we were close to a forest. "Is this our last stop?" we wondered. "Is this where we will be taken to be shot in the woods?"

Then the soldiers just left us standing in an empty field close to the woods. They ran off to save their own lives.

We prisoners stood together afraid to move. Suddenly everyone was shouting out different ideas of what we should do. "Stay"..."Don't move"..."Run"...Let's separate"..."Let's run in different directions."

Some thought that if the Nazis still wanted to kill us we should make them come and search for us, instead of just standing there. So we started running in all directions, still not knowing what would happen to us if we were captured by the SS.

One of my friends asked me to join the group that she was escaping with, but I refused. I thought her group was too big. Alone, I ran off into the woods, hoping to survive there. I decided to depend on my own instincts and my own strong will to live.

It was very scary being alone in the woods. When I heard a noise I thought that either there were still German troops hiding in the forest, or that there might be a wild animal after me. I stopped to listen and then I started walking fast, almost running, afraid for my life.

Deep in the woods I heard people speaking Polish. I ran towards their voices. I found them to be Poles who had been deported to Germany to provide labor for a big German farm.   When the German farmer and his family abandoned the farm and ran to save themselves from the approaching Russian army, these Poles were left at the farm.

I stayed with that group of Poles and also some Russian workers in the barn. During the night we heard gun shots. Bombs exploded all through the night. We were fearful that one of the bombs would strike the barn and we would all be killed. It was a frightening experience to be at the front line of the war where the Russians were engaging the Germans in battle.

I had survived all of the atrocities of the concentration camps, and here I was, still in danger. I was scared by the gunshots, not knowing where they were being fired from, or where the bullets might strike.

Then came the dawn, and with the morning light we heard the sound of tanks approaching our barn. Russian soldiers accompanied those tanks, and they told us that we were free. The Polish workers, Russian workers and I, the one Jewish survivor from the death camp, looked at each other in disbelief and then started hugging and kissing, shouting, "We are alive. We are free." "No more Germans with the guns who had power over our lives." We were free. The Russians liberated us.

The American, British and French armies soon approached from the other side. The date was May 8, 1945, and it marked the end of World War II. On that day a peace accord was signed between the Allied forces and Germany. And on that day, I was free.

I had lived to see the fall of Germany under Hitler's Nazi regime.

CHAPTER 12

LIBERATION—1945

When I was in Birkenau living in misery, I thought a lot about revenge. I witnessed what was going on around me, and I was grieving for my family. In my thoughts I saw myself doing to the German people all the horrible things that were done to us.

I thought about revenge: revenge for the death of my family, relatives and others, revenge for our humiliation and suffering, and revenge for my wasted young years.

When it came closer to liberation, I heard the bombs falling on their cities, and I saw German people on the roads, running scared for their lives, and the soldiers pulling back. I felt relief that they were being punished for allowing Hitler's Nazi regime and his followers to commit all those exterminations and inhumane treatment against the Jewish people.

After the liberation, I could not have hurt anybody to take revenge. I believe that I am not capable of killing innocent people. I was taught tolerance, not hatred and killing. Hitler and his Nazi chief operators were concentrating on the extermination of all Jewish people and others. They were geniuses of death. They knew how to kill. They were expert in it.

It was hard to believe that I was free, that I could go wherever I wanted without German soldiers watching over me. I was alive and free, but my sister Hilda did not survive. For the first time, I asked myself, "How was I able to survive the Holocaust and she and others did not?" "Why me?" It was a happy and a sad time for me.

I wanted to get out of Germany and get to Poland and my hometown of Radziejow, with hopes of finding someone from my family alive. But it wasn't so easy.

The Russians liberated us, and they needed people to do some work for them. There were no German people around because they had all run away from the village from the approaching Russian army. So, we were taken to work. If we refused, we were told, "We liberated you. You worked for the Germans. Now you can work for us." We had no choice, so we had to.

We had to clean the dirt and debris caused by the fighting between the German and the Russian armies. We were supervised by the Russian soldiers. Some of them wanted to take advantage of us, the two girls, but we were protected by the ten men in our group.

Among our group there was a father and his 12 year old son. The father got close to the Russian girl and the son was left to take care of himself. When I joined the group, I felt sorry for the young boy and took care of him. For my kindness to the boy, I got respect from the whole group.

After the work was done, while we were still staying in the farmer's house, we made our plans of what to do next. The men got a big wagon and two horses and we started our journey back to Poland. We were traveling through towns in Germany during the day and stopping to rest in abandoned German houses during the night.

While traveling with the group of Polish and Russian workers, we stopped for a rest in one of the abandoned homes of some German people. The Russian girl and I were busy preparing dinner for the group. After dinner, some Russian soldiers came to the house. They brought some vodka and played the harmonica and made themselves at home. They stayed for awhile and then they left. Two officers who were dressed nicely came back later and conversed with the Russian people. When it got late, we all prepared ourselves for a night's rest, to be ready in the morning to continue our journey closer to the Polish border. At that time, I got rid of my camp clothes. I found a pair of slacks and a top. They were my only clothes for the day and night to sleep in.

In the attic of the house, there was a bed where I went to sleep. Close by, the others of the group were resting, as well as the two Russian officers who made themselves comfortable on the floor for the night.

One of the officers came and sat on my bed and started to make passes at me. He was a pilot and promised to fly me back to Poland. Realizing that I was in a bad situation, I begged him to leave me alone, that I was a concentration camp survivor and sick to my stomach. When that did not work, I jumped out of the bed, ran to the dark corner of the attic, stuck a finger in my throat and forced myself to throw up. Not knowing where to hide from him, afraid, I returned back to my bed and begged him again to leave me alone. He took out the gun from his holster and put it next to me on the pillow. Scared to death, unsure of what to do next, I started to cry. When that did not convince him to leave me alone, I repeated my trick a few more times. It felt like it went on forever. Here again I was feeling hopeless, threatened with a gun, if I would not submit to his wishes.

I had survived the war and all those camps and came out alive. Here I was in a situation, again scared to death, afraid to get some disease or have a baby with a Russian officer. I was a survivor, skin and bones, and intimacy was the last thing on my mind. I was making so much noise going back and forth, that I woke up the people sleeping nearby.

The other Russian officer woke up, came to my bed and spoke to his friend. He said, "I saw this poor skinny Jewish girl, with her number on her arm and I did not want to take advantage of her." Then he told him to leave the house right away. To me he said, "I am a doctor. I want you to come to our station in the morning, and I will give you some medication to settle your stomach." Then, they both left. All the other men from the group could not believe the trick that I played on the officer. When it got light in the morning, we quietly left the town.

On our journey back to Poland, we came upon other survivors from my last camp. They were by themselves or in a group. Some of them wanted to join us but there was no room for them in the wagon. We also met some other girls on their way back to different parts of Poland, Czechoslovakia, and other European countries.

After traveling together with the group for over a week, we all separated close to the Polish border. Each of us went our separate ways back to our hometowns. In my group heading back home was a Polish man who lived close to our town. He assured me that he would take care of me to get me home. We made plans to travel together. I helped him carry some of the possessions that he accumulated in Germany.

We went to an office where we received some food and a ticket to travel back to Poland. I recall we ended up on some train which was just a platform on which we traveled for hours. The trains were full of Jewish prisoners and Polish workers returning to their homeland. Then the two of us changed to a passenger train which took us to a station close to our towns. We separated and he went to Pieterkow Kuj.

I stopped by a Polish farmer who had been a customer of ours before the war. He had such a lovely family and we were so close to them. They were shocked to see me. They asked about the rest of my family. At that time, I had no answer. They invited me to have dinner with them and told me that a few survivors had come back to Radziejow.

After dinner, they drove me to Radziejow with some fresh produce and a feather pillow.

CHAPTER 13

BACK IN RADZIEJOW—1945

When I arrived in my hometown of Radziejow, I was hoping to find someone alive from my family. But unfortunately, I found out with horror that they all perished.

No one else survived.

It was the worst time of my entire life. I was left alone. I missed my family so much and I was very lonely. Always questioning, "Why me? Why am I alive? Why was I spared? Why did I survive and they did not?"

For my family, the liberation came too late.

I did meet about ten other survivors and we stayed together in a Jewish family's big house. None of the people who owned the home survived. We took care of each other like a family.

I came back to Radziejow six years older since the German invasion of Poland. I was 24 years old without a family, homeless, almost toothless, and limping.

The house my family owned was now occupied by Polish people.

A few times I walked by the house where my family lived. This was so painful, but it also brought back many good memories. In my mind I could see my family gather at the Friday night dinner table with my father sitting at the head of the table enjoying the meal with my mother and the children. He would sing in his beautiful voice all kinds of religious songs. I could also envision my brothers and sisters with my mother. She was mixing a bowl of egg yolks with sugar, and if one of the children had a cold and was coughing, we all had to have a portion of the mixture (medicine).

And then in my mind I could see the little ducks running around in our back yard and the children laughing and having so much fun playing with them.

So many memories and nobody was in the house. Where were they? How could a thing like this happen? It was unbelievable. I felt like I was living in a bad dream.

The door of our store was closed and it felt so quiet. I could not walk up the steps, could not make myself go in there.

I did not care to ask for the things which were left in the house. Possessions? Who needed them? Even being free was hard to get used to. After six years under Hitler's Nazi ruling, I forgot what normal life was. Material things were not important to me. I was mourning for my family and the rest did not matter.

We were hoping some more survivors would come back to our town looking for their families, but unfortunately, not too many people from our town came back.

We were not welcome in our home town either. Some of the Jewish people of Radziejow were well-off and lived in well built houses with nice furniture. Those who came back to reclaim their properties were not welcomed because those houses were now occupied by Polish people. They thought that now everything belonged to them.

We did not stay too long in Radziejow because the Polish underground, antisemitic groups, tried to kill us survivors. There was a small town nearby called Osieczyny, where a father and son who survived the war were killed.

We felt as though we didn't belong in our town anymore. The two temples had been burned down. All the houses where Jewish people lived were now occupied by Polish people. So many familiar faces were gone. They were all killed. The Jewish community of Radziejow was gone forever.

After a few weeks, we all left our hometown. It was very sad. Not one Jewish person was left living in Radziejow.

I went to Czestochowa and stayed for a short while with some people from Radziejow. We occupied ourselves by visiting all the places where the Holocaust survivors now gathered. We went to look for the names of missing relatives and familiar faces. We also looked at the bulletin boards for the names of people that survived hoping to find the name of a relative.

I met my girlfriend Yetta in Czestochowa. She brought back good memories for me from our teen years. Back in our youth, we were a group of six girlfriends who I shared my free time with. This friend Yetta and I were together in Lojewo, and she is also the one that I hid with in the attic. She eventually immigrated to Australia. We still keep in contact with one other. Another girlfriend, Iska, survived Birkenau. A third girlfriend, Regina, was taken to Birkenau on another transport. We were so shocked to see each other there. She was the prettiest girl in our town. When I met her in Birkenau, I hardly recognized her. She was a skeleton and very sick. I never saw her again. She did not survive. My fourth girlfriend, Rushka, did not survive. She was caught by the Gestapo and shot. My fifth girlfriend, Salle, also did not survive. I never found out what happened to her or how she perished in the Holocaust.

Walking in Czestochowa, I also came across a group of survivors, young girls and boys. Their plans were to travel to Palestine. They tried to convince me to go with them. I was confused about what to do. As a teenager before the war, I belonged to a Zionist organization and my dream was to immigrate to Palestine, but now I could not make up my mind.

I knew at that time that there were papers, visas, for me in Germany to go to America. I knew that my Uncle Israel and Auntie Mania and cousins who I grew up with were waiting for me to come. I also had two other uncles, Max and Sam, the Levy brothers, who sent a visa for me to come to the United States. They had families there also. I was desperately looking for a family. I was always surrounded by my loving parents, brothers and sisters, and here I was all alone.

I was at a crossroads and not able to make up my mind. Should I choose my dream of going to Palestine or to family in America? My loneliness won. I told the group of survivors that I would be going to my family in America.

"Tell Me Where Should I Go?" Later, when I heard this English and Yiddish song sung by Steve Lawrence, my tears would always come.

CHAPTER 14

BACK TO GERMANY

I made plans to go back to Germany to inquire about my visa to the United States. I joined a group of about ten people. We had small bags that we carried with us and we traveled on foot, hoping to get rides from other travelers. We were stopped by a few Russian soldiers traveling the route with a wagon. Poland at that time was occupied by the Russians. They offered us a ride which we were happy to accept. We were so tired from walking. We all piled into the wagon with our small possessions. After traveling with them for a few miles, they stopped the wagon and demanded that we get out and leave all of our belongings in the wagon. They had guns and we were helpless. Once again, we were left with only the clothes we had on our bodies.

In the group was also my cousin, Ben Neuman, who survived the Holocaust, the only survivor from my many cousins. After liberation, he joined the police in Poland in Aleksandrow. After working there for awhile he feared for his life and had to run away. He joined our group going to Germany. He eventually immigrated to the United States where he had two brothers. We were very close. We always tried to help each other during the war and in the displaced persons camp. Unfortunately, he passed away in 2002.

After being in Germany for a short time, someone told me that they saw one of my brothers, Bernard, in Poland. We still had no possessions and no home. I went with another group of survivors back to Poland. I looked all over Poland, but did not find my brother Bernard who supposedly survived Chelmno.

After traveling in Poland, we decided again to cross the border into Germany. This time we traveled by train back to Germany. This was the last time I saw Poland, and I never looked back.

We couldn't find a place to settle down. Israel at that time was not yet a state, and the immigration to other countries was very slow.

Back in Germany, I lived in a displaced persons (DP) camp in Bergen-Belsen. During the war it was occupied by SS and Gestapo. It was also not far from the Bergen-Belsen Concentration and death camp where thousands of people lost their lives, including Anne Frank.

Here again we were visiting the clubhouse, reading the bulletin boards, hoping to find a familiar name on it. I was not ready to give up yet, and always hoping maybe somebody did survive. But unfortunately there was nobody from my family on it. They were all gone. I was left all alone to take care of myself.

In the DP camp, I lived in a large room with three other survivors. All of us came from Radziejow—my cousin Ben, his cousin Manes, a friend Luba and I. We had four army beds which we divided with sheets for privacy. Each one of us had an Army metal closet. In the middle of the room was a table and chair, and in the corner was a tiny kitchen.

We were mostly single people liberated from the concentration and death camps who had lost our families, and we were lonely. After awhile, we were looking for someone to share our lives with. Weddings were performed almost every day. The wedding gowns were lent to us by a group of religious women and they were fitted as needed to the proper size.

I met my future husband, Michael, there; he was also a survivor from my hometown, Radziejow. We fell in love and got married in Germany in October of 1946. There was no one from my family to attend. Our wedding was performed by Rabbi Olewski, who was a Rabbi in Celle. He was also a friend of my father's. Our wedding took place in the same room we lived in. After we got married, my single bed was exchanged for a bunk bed.

In the DP camp of Bergen-Belsen life slowly started to normalize. Instead of waiting in line for soup to be rationed out, we started to cook our own meals. People began to be paid for the work they did in the camp. I received some packages from my family in America. The coffee they sent me was exchanged for fruit, vegetables and other goods.

School opened so the children that survived could receive some education. People were taught professions. Children were born while we were waiting for immigration papers to leave Germany and enter other countries.

The birth of our son Harold in 1948 was such an unbelievable experience filled with happiness. The woman who gave birth to this baby was not supposed to survive. She was sentenced to death, and against all odds brought new life to this world. We named him after our fathers. Harold was a beautiful baby. When he was born I received a beautiful complete layette from my family in America. He was the best dressed baby in Bergen-Belsen.

CHAPTER 15

UNITED STATES—1949

We finely came to the United States in 1949. We ended up in Milwaukee, Wisconsin, where my family lived. My mother had three brothers there. Michael and I raised three beautiful children, our son Harold, and daughters, Gilda, born in 1950, and Sally, born in 1957. Both girls were born in Milwaukee.

When Gilda was born, the doctor came in my room and told me, "You have a healthy, beautiful baby girl." I felt like the luckiest woman. We named her after our deceased mothers. When Sally was born, our son had wanted a brother, and our daughter wanted a sister, but we were all very happy with the addition to our family. We all adored her. She was our baby. She was beautiful and we loved her very much. We named her after my husband's sister and my grandmother.

When we arrived in the United States I didn't feel like talking about the Holocaust. There was the language barrier and I felt like an outsider. The only people I felt comfortable with were the survivors that had been there. We could understand each other and developed a strong bond and felt like a family.

Living in the United States, but not knowing how to speak English, Michael got a job at a factory and I stayed home raising our children. We also attended night school to learn the English language.

After being in the United States for five years, we became U.S. citizens. I changed my first name from Jetka to Joyce, which was easier to spell and pronounce.

After learning the language, we bought a small grocery store where we worked 7 days a week from 7:00 in the morning until 9:00 at night. We also became very patriotic and we never missed voting in an election. For a special occasion, we purchased U.S. Savings Bonds as a gift.

I recall one of my proudest moments was when we had an Israeli Bond drive. We did not yet have a checking account, but we wanted to buy our first Israeli Bond. I went with my husband with one hundred single dollar bills from the day's sales at the grocery store and brought them to the temple where the drive was taking place. The people in charge of the bond drive looked at us with admiration. For my husband and me, this was a proud accomplishment that we were able to make a small contribution to the State of Israel. It felt good. It was an important event in the Jewish community of Milwaukee where the Jewish-American actor George Jessel and the comedienne Phyllis Diller entertained us.

Michael was a very devoted husband and father who loved us dearly. We worked very hard to give our children a good home life and a good education. Our life in America was peaceful.

Then Michael got sick and was diagnosed with hardening of the arteries by a doctor in Milwaukee. Hoping the warm weather would improve his condition, we moved to Florida in 1976. Shortly thereafter while taking a drive to a local store Michael got confused and tried to drive back home—to Milwaukee. After reporting him missing to the police, they found him twenty-four hours later, more than 100 miles from home.

He was later examined and again, diagnosed with having hardening of the arteries.

Several months later when visiting Chicago, a doctor determined that his condition was Alzheimer's disease. That was in 1976, he was only in his mid-sixties. There was little information and no resources or support for caregivers of Alzheimer's patients.

Once I was sitting at a table with other people when the sweet rolls and coffee were brought. My husband wanted all the sweet rolls for himself. Being embarrassed, I told them, "My husband is a sick man." I apologized to the people and we left the table. If I would have said the word "Alzheimers" then, they might have thought he had a contagious disease since so little was known of the illness at that time.

Why him? He was full of life, loved having people all around him, always telling jokes and he had a terrific memory. And with this illness his grandson became his son, and I became "the lady who brought food for him and fed him".

With his illness my life revolved around my husband. I took care of him the best I could. The love for my husband, and the love from my children, and the admiration from friends and people around me, kept me going for ten years of his confinement in a nursing home.

After being ill for so long, he passed away in 1988.

Although the later part of my life has been filled with happiness from my children and 9 grandchildren, as long as I live, I will never forget what I went through during Hitler's Nazi regime and what I lost.

I am the only survivor of my family, and many aunts, uncles and cousins. My parents and two younger sisters, Chaya and Hava, after staying in Klobuck almost a year, were sent to Treblinka death camp. My brother Shlomo was sent to a prison camp in Pozen not because he did anything wrong; his crime was being Jewish. He did not survive. My brother Bernard, who ran from the attic where we were hiding, into the basement, was caught and murdered with the other Jews from our town in Chelmno. My third brother, Shymek, who was on the transport with me to Auschwitz, died in the men's camp from starvation or typhus—I don't know for sure. And my sister Hilda who was with me in Auschwitz died from the typhus epidemic.

I loved my family very dearly, and after so many years I still miss them all very much. My family has no graves. Their bones and ashes are spread over Auschwitz-Birkenau, Chelmno, Treblinka, and Pozen.

I still often ask myself, "Why me? Why did I survive?" I can't believe it myself.

Some people say somebody was watching over me. Why then me and not the others?

Still, when I walk in the streets, I look at faces, hoping, maybe by some miracle, I will recognize somebody. But they are not there. I can't and won't forget them.

I try not to live in the past but the past lives in me.

This is a very tragic story but it had to be told. The injustices done to the Jewish people during Hitler's regime should not be forgotten. People who survived have the responsibility to tell their story of what happened in the mass murder camps, and the cruelty and barbaric acts of Hitler's followers, the SS men and the Gestapo.

We must not forget the six million Jews who perished in the Holocaust, one and a half million of whom were innocent children, and the millions of non-Jews who also perished at this time. This is what hatred can do.

I was there. I am a survivor of Auschwitz-Birkenau, Ravensbrueck, Mecklenburg, Lojewo and smaller camps. I survived to tell about this horrible time in my life. These horrible memories will haunt me for the rest of my life.

To survive I also had to be a fighter—not as a ghetto fighter or as a partisan who fought in the forest to survive. I fought not to lose my faith and not to give up. I fought to stay alive to keep my promise to bear witness to the cruelty of Hitler's regime. I survived by luck and miracles. I also believe in fate. I was skin and bones and yet here I was among the living. When I recall Auschwitz-Birkenau, the other camps, and the death march, I know it was almost impossible to survive. I was living one day at a time.

When one lost the will to live, or gave up, death would follow. I still had faith that somebody was watching over me.

I have spent my whole life trying to forget and finally realized that I never can forget the horror that I witnessed and endured. I grieve for the tremendous loss of my loved ones. One mourns if someone in the family dies, but it's worse when they die so young and tragically.

Every survivor has a tragic story to tell, and this is only part of my story. The will and need to bear witness is very important to me, and the promise some of us made to each other is my promise kept.

The dead cannot speak.

We must learn from history and the lessons of the past.

I have read some books about the Holocaust and about different camps. Some of the survivors had positions in the camps or were helped by others, and still had to have luck to survive.

Comparing myself to them, I had no position in the camps and I had nobody to help me. I was just a prisoner who lived from day to day and miraculously survived the many camps, Auschwitz-Birkenau, and the death march. I still cannot imagine how I made it or anyone else. It is beyond belief.

I like to listen to other survivors and hear about their experiences during Hitler's regime and how they survived. I met one woman at a sisterhood meeting at my synagogue. We started a conversation about the video I made for the Shoah Foundation. She wanted to see it, and she came to my apartment with her younger sister, both survivors of Birkenau.

Watching the video, they could not get over how similar some of our experiences were. She also was the older sister who took care of her younger sister. She also speaks to students about her experiences. Her sister cannot do it. She was asked to light a candle on Yom Hashoah, the Holocaust Memorial Day, and she refused. It is too painful for her.

Another time, at a Yom Hashoah, Holocaust Remembrance memorial ceremony sponsored by the B'nai B'rith Organization, titled "Unto every person there is a name," I was asked to read the names of my family who were killed in the Holocaust and speak about our experiences. After the ceremony, two women, Holocaust survivors, came over and thanked me for my words because they could not do it themselves.

Maybe I too wouldn't be able to speak publicly about my experiences but my daughter Gilda, a high school counselor, encourages me to do it. The will to speak and tell my story is very strong in me and as long as people are interested in listening, I will continue. Even though I once had a bad experience speaking to a whole auditorium of high school students in Wheaton, Illinois, when my mind went blank (thank God nobody noticed it). When I recovered, I was able to continue with my speech.

Once, after speaking to some high school students, I came home to flowers and a thank-you note from a parent. Another time after I spoke, one parent called my daughter to tell her that the conversation at the dinner table was about the Holocaust, and that nobody was in a hurry to leave the table that night. This gives me courage to continue to speak and educate the students about the Holocaust, even though it is increasingly more difficult each time.

When I speak to high school students as part of their history studies of the Holocaust, I allow time for questions and answers. I also receive thank-you letters from the students with sympathetic comments and more questions. Some questions that stand out in my mind which I will attempt to answer are:

1) "How come you didn't cry when your sister died?"

2) "How did you live with one another in the camps?"

3) "How is your faith after the Holocaust?"

4) "How did it affect your life?

"How come I didn't cry?" Nobody can imagine why I did not cry when my sister died in her sleep. You had to be there to understand the feelings. When you saw what was going on in Birkenau: we were all skin and bones, working all the time, and thinking about when your time would be up and whether you would die by shooting, starvation, being beaten to death, or taken to the gas chambers. We never knew what was about to happen to us. We prisoners sometimes envied the dead. We lived in a place where nobody expected to survive.

There was no hope to survive the hell of Auschwitz-Birkenau.

As time went on and I remained alive, I started crying and questioning, "Why did she have to die while I was still alive?" I miss my sister very much. She was so young. When I think of her, tears always come to my eyes.

In Birkenau, we cried all the time. I cried when I was hungry thinking back to when my mother sat at our table forcing us children to eat our meal. I cried when we walked to work in the snow on cold winter days with very little clothes to keep us warm. I cried looking at the tall chimney with the smoke and fire coming out of it and thinking of those innocent people turning to ashes. I cried thinking of my family, where they were, and what conditions they were living in, or were they even still alive?

"How did we live with one another at the camp?" There were some with whom we shared an extra crumb of bread. There were others who couldn't wait for another prisoner to die so they could take their wooden shoes and every belonging from them.

We had to be very careful of what we had. We couldn't leave a piece of bread on our bunk bed to save for later when we came back from work because it would be stolen or eaten by rats. Whatever we had on our bodies and in our stomach was ours.

When we first came to Birkenau, we were crowded in, 10 people to a bunk bed. After a few months, there were five of us left.

There was a mother, Machela, her older daughter Regina, and her younger daughter Jenny, my younger sister Hilda, and me. It felt good having somebody older than me to listen to for a change. When the mother got a piece of extra bread, she shared it with her two daughters, my sister, and me. She was a very generous person. I met so many other girls in the barracks and at the working places, but these three women will always remain so vivid in my memories. She survived Auschwitz with her two daughters. After the liberation she left for Israel and somehow she found out that I also survived and that I was in the Bergen Belsen DP, displaced person's camp. She sent me a package of fruit from Israel to Germany. After I came to the United States, I lost contact with her but I will never forget her, this generous woman whom I met in Auschwitz.

"How is my faith after the Holocaust?" Do I still believe in God after going through so much in the Holocaust?" My parents were religious people and I was brought up in a religious home. I keep a traditional (kosher) home and I believe there is a God. But when the question of God and the Holocaust comes up, I have mixed feelings.

In my mind I question why God allowed 6 million Jewish people to be killed. And then, I remind myself about my father who taught us children that God is always right and we should not question Him. Then I feel guilty to be asking "Why?"

"How did it affect my life?" The malnutrition was so bad in Birkenau that I got sores in my mouth and my teeth started falling out. I did not have to pull them out, I just spit them out. I had two upper teeth left and a few lower ones. The first upper dentures I got were in Celle, a small town in Germany, when I was still single. I also couldn't get around so easy. I was still limping and I forced myself not to be tied down.

After the war, when I started eating, I got sick with dysentery and had to start my intake of food gradually. When I felt better, I could not stop eating.

I remember one day sitting at our dinner table in Radziejow a few weeks after liberation. We had chicken soup with noodles for dinner. I filled my plate with soup and noodles. One of my friends, Roman, put a spoon in the plate; the spoon stood straight up and did not fall down. That's how thick the soup was! We all had a good laugh at the table but it wasn't funny. I started gaining weight, and having a small frame, the weight started to interfere with my health. I tired easily. I went on a diet though I didn't know what was good for me and what not to eat. I started skipping dinners. I lost the weight but my health never improved.

All my life, I've suffered from a bad stomach. I've gone to the largest medical centers in the United States where the doctors look at me, learn that I am a Holocaust survivor, and always give me the same diagnosis, a nervous stomach. I'm supposed to live with that.

In the beginning, after liberation, I covered the number on my arm with a bandage. My arm was so sore from the constant bandages that my skin started bleeding. Then I started wearing long-sleeved blouses, even in the hot weather in Florida.

I was once given the offer by a plastic surgeon to remove my number for no charge, but I couldn't do it, even for free. Even though it's hard to look at, it is a constant connection with my family.

I have trouble falling asleep every night because that's the time I think the most about the Holocaust and my family. I can't help it. It sometimes feels like I am still there.

To this day, I have guilty feelings and I cannot forget the words of my younger sister Hava. When I sent her away to the Protectorate to be safer, she was crying and said to me, "I don't want to go away. I want to go with you. You want to live. I want to live too." When I think of her, tears always come to my eyes. Thinking of the tragic moment when she was forced to the gas chambers of Treblinka and choking to death.

Why didn't I let her stay with me? They might have survived. At that time it looked very bleak. But when I meet younger survivors from Birkenau, I think about my sisters and wonder if they too could have survived if they had stayed with me. Then my thoughts go back to my arrival in Auschwitz and the selection where I would have had in front of me three sisters, 11 years, 12 years and 14 years of age. There was no chance that Dr. Mengele would let all of us go to the right side. I would not want to be separated from them, would have followed them, and all of us would be sent to the left, straight to the gas chambers.

Maybe I was destined to survive to keep the memory of my family alive so they would not be forgotten like they never existed. Sometimes I just want to make some sense of all of this, of this tragic situation we were all forced into.

During the day, I try to keep busy. When I don't feel well or feel depressed, I try to get out of the house and be among people. Reading is also good therapy for me. I call this my best medicine.

Every survivor is an individual who handles his past differently. No two stories of survival are the same and not everybody had the same experiences.

After the liberation, we lived in a DP camp in Germany waiting for the visa to clear for my husband, my son, and myself to come to the United States. While living in Germany, I had to put iron bars on my windows. I had awful nightmares that the Gestapo were coming to take my child away. Those awful dreams continue to this day, but here, when those dreams wake me up, I remind myself that I am in the United States and that my family is safe. Even so many years after the war, those nightmares are still haunting me.

Later, when I was raising my children, I was a nervous parent. When my children were in their teens, when they went out on a date, I stayed up until they came home, always especially cautious about their safety. I worried about them a lot and was very overprotective of them.

My older daughter, Gilda, was playing outside with her friend when she was 5 years old. When her friend's grandmother walked by, my daughter ran to her and called her "Grandma." Her friend told her, "She's not your grandmother, she's mine." That's how children sometimes act. Gilda came running to the house crying about what her friend said and wanted to know, "Where is my grandmother?" To protect her, I told her that her friend was wrong. How do you explain to a 5 year-old what really happened to her grandmother?

Some friends talk about their families, and how they spend their time and celebrations together. I listen to them and I am happy for them but it hurts also. Where is my family? Why didn't I have the pleasure of celebrating happy occasions with siblings, and nieces and nephews? My children also felt that something was missing.

When my children got older, they knew that there was a difference between their own family and their friends' families. There were no grandparents on either side and no cousins. We didn't discuss this openly with them because it was too painful.

When my daughter Gilda came home from high school crying that her boyfriend asked someone else to the prom and not her, I reprimanded her to stop her from crying. I told her, "There are more important things to cry about in our house." That's when the tragedy of the Holocaust came out in our family, and I started to talk about my experiences during World War II.

There is a saying that time heals, but that is not how it is with me. When I was younger, my time was occupied with my children and helping my husband with the business. After my husband passed away, while living alone, my thoughts always go back to the past, my youth, my family and those horrible times in Hitler's regime.

When a piece of bread gets stale, how can you throw it away in the garbage? I have strong memories when we were starving for a piece of bread. There are so many bad memories; it's impossible to forget. I will always be grateful to my children, my husband and my work to keep me occupied, to keep my sanity and keep me from depression.

When I think back to those nameless people I met in Birkenau and Mecklenburg (many whose names I cannot remember from so long ago) who did not survive, it is so sad. The beautiful girl from Lodz who worked next to my machine in the Union factory; we became so fond of each other; and this Jewish man from Greece who also worked nearby. Whenever he spoke to her, you could see the love in his eyes that he had for her. When she was taken away by a selection to the gas chambers, he was so heartbroken. After a few days, he also did not come back to work and I never saw him again. This good-looking man from Greece went through sterilization in Dr. Mengele's laboratory.

I remember the intelligent girl who I worked with in Mecklenburg. You could see she came from a caring home with a good education. She was very quiet, and I hardly ever saw a smile on her face. She never wanted to talk about her family. Sometimes I think, maybe she lost a husband and a child and it was just too painful for her to talk about it. She was such a refined person. We never had an argument and got along so nicely, working together just the two of us. We shared our workload and our food. We were separated and never saw each other again. Did she survive? And all those other young girls I got to know. Did they survive?

After so many years, I am still haunted by these awful memories. The whistle of a train brings back memories of my arrival to Auschwitz and all the transports of people arriving from all over Europe. The vision of a tall chimney brings back memories of the crematoria with the smoke and fire coming out and the awful stink of burning flesh.

After being in the United States for more than 10 years, we bought a house that was across the street from a school. The chimney of this school was so tall that every morning I hated to raise the shades of the windows and look at it. The chimney always reminded me of Birkenau. After three years, we sold the house and moved into a smaller place behind our business where I was not afraid to open my shades.

I am often asked if I went back to Auschwitz after liberation. I just couldn't go back to see the mountains of hair, the shoes, the eyeglasses, the baby pacifiers, and other items displayed there in the exhibits in some of the barracks. I saw those items on the people going to the gas chambers. It would be too painful; too many bad memories. But it is very important for people, especially young people, to see it—to see the extraordinary conditions we lived in and how people were sadistically killed.

I had an experience recently that led to a sad realization. I was an outpatient at the hospital and the nurse who was taking care of me noticed the tattooed number on my arm. She looked at me and said sadly, "You don't see too many people left with numbers on their arms." I realized that she was right.

There are fewer and fewer of us eyewitnesses alive everyday. That is why it is so important for me to share my story so people will know what really happened in the Holocaust and at Auschwitz-Birkenau, the largest graveyard of human ashes in the history of the world.

We survived to bear witness to the destruction of 6 million Jewish people and millions of others. This should never happen again to anyone in the world. Never again.

Never forget.

Some Neo-Nazis and other antisemitic people, Holocaust deniers, claim that the Holocaust never happened. But tragically these atrocities did happen.

I lived the tragedy. I was there.

CHAPTER 16

AFTERWARDS

My experiences also have had a big effect on my children and grandchildren. When I visited my son Harold's family and his triplets were little, Brittany, Brent and Brandon always questioned the number on my arm. Their older brother Michael tried to explain to them about the bad people who tried to hurt grandma. When Michael was 13 years old, I went to his Hebrew class to speak to the students about the Holocaust. After speaking, I received a phone call from a parent telling me how appreciative the students were.

When my other grandson Michael was 6 years old, he tried to rub the ugly number off my arm. When that didn't work, he took a bar of soap and tried to wash it off. Finally, he kissed my arm to make me feel better because some bad people stuck pins in grandma's arm to hurt her, and he wanted to take away the pain. After each kiss, he repeated, "Does that feel better grandma?"

When Michael was in grade school, the students learned about Martin Luther King and about slavery. He raised his hand to tell the teacher and the class about his grandmother being a slave. He begged the teacher to let him bring his grandma to school for "show and tell." I had to visit his class to show the students my number that I received as a slave, when "the bad man" Hitler was in power. How do you explain to 6-year-old children about the Holocaust? It wasn't easy.

When my granddaughter Hilary was in second grade, she had to make a project for the class. Her project was, "My Special Grandmother." She outlined a hand, and on it drew my concentration camp number, 57779, with the upside-down triangle, and wrote a part of my Holocaust story. She finished it with, "I am proud to be named Hilary, after my grandmother's three younger sisters who died in the Holocaust, Haya, Hava, and Hilda."

When my grandson Eddie was 9 years old, he entered a contest, for the 1988-89, National PTA Reflections Program, on his proud experiences. This is what he wrote with a picture of me:

> This is my grandma Joyce, and I am proud of her because she is what you call a survivor. When she was 18 years old, the Nazi German soldiers came to her town in Poland. All the Jewish people were loaded on to trains and taken to camps. These camps my grandma told me about were called concentration camps, and people were being killed there. My grandma got a number on her arm. The young and strong people were needed to work as slaves, so that is what my grandma did. She built roads. But six of her brothers and sisters, and parents and grandparents died there. My grandma was the only one who lived because she was brave and strong and she wouldn't give up. My mom and sister and I wouldn't even be here if she didn't survive. And that's why I am so proud of my grandma. She is a superhero.

My granddaughter Rachel is sensitive to my past experience. She also questioned the number on my arm when she was younger and has read many books related to the Holocaust. Her younger sister, Deena, is too young to comprehend all that happened; though she also feels bad about the number on her grandma's arm and knows it is related to the war.

My youngest daughter, Sally, was very sensitive to my feelings. She felt bad for what I went through, and tried not to make it worse. She avoided bringing up problems to protect me and tried to keep me happy as much as possible. She would share the good things and try to spare me the bad.

My two daughters had an understanding not to bring up bad things with me because of what I went through in the Holocaust.

My daughter Sally, as a high school student at John Marshall in Milwaukee, had to do an assignment for a class. I remember as we traveled on a two-hour bus ride to Kenosha, Wisconsin, where my husband had his last business, she interviewed me and wrote a six-page paper about my experience in the Holocaust. She was happy to have at least a short version of my story on paper.

Sally also helped me to transcribe my written words onto the computer. We enjoyed working together on this project which spread out over a number of years. By working together she understood more of what I went through and what the Holocaust meant to me. It brought us even closer together.

My daughter Gilda, as a guidance counselor at a high school in Glen Ellyn, Illinois, took part in a collection of writings by faculty and staff in 1997. Here is what she wrote:

Untitled by Gilda Ross

For as far back as I can remember, I knew my parents were different. I'm sure all children feel that at one time or another, but that's not what I'm talking about. Perhaps it had something to do with their extremes of emotion. All parents worry, but not all parents sell their home and move across town when one of their children is involved in a neighborhood spat. And I'm not sure when I first became aware of their "history," but I knew the usual tragedies of childhood and adolescence were not to be tolerated. My mother had lived the "tragedy." Having your boyfriend ask a different girl to the prom was not a "tragedy."

She never talked about the tattooed number on her arm but consistently nursed the irritated skin the Band-Aid covering it up would cause. She never wanted anyone to ask her about her number. It would stir up too many memories, she would say. She never considered having it removed by plastic surgery. She knew that would never erase the painful memories.

It was while I worked as a counselor at Glenbard North in Carol Stream, Illinois, in 1977, that I first asked her to speak about her past. The school play that year was "The Diary of Anne Frank." I knew she could offer special insights.

And as we held hands, she began:

"I came from a large and happy family that included my nine sisters and brothers, aunts and uncles, and grandparents, and I was the only member of my family to survive the Holocaust. I was 18 when the Nazis invaded our small town in Poland and 24 when I was liberated from Auschwitz...."As she continued to talk, her voice became less and less shaky.

Every spring my Mom comes to visit me from Florida. And every spring my mother speaks to hundreds of DuPage-area high school students about what can happen when the world goes mad.

My son Harold also had some thoughts to be included in this book. He wrote:

I am the oldest child of Joyce and Michael Wagner. Being the first-born child of Holocaust survivors brought with it great appreciation and great sorrow.

Knowing what my parents endured was never an easy thing to understand. Even after hearing the horrible stories, it was impossible to truly comprehend what it must have actually felt like to be there and live through the hell of the Holocaust.

Every day my mother told me how lucky I was to be alive. My father worked harder then any parent I knew to give our family a good life.

I will forever thank my father for all my success in life today. Had he lived longer I know he would be proud of the man I've become.

I will forever thank my mother for instilling in me a passion for life and even more importantly, an appreciation for God and our religion. Without her unbelievable will to live and her refusal to ever give up, I know I wouldn't be writing this today

I love you mom and dad. I promise your memories will live on forever in your children, grandchildren and your future great grandchildren. We will all never forget.

Every year when I am the speaker at the Yom Hashoah Holocaust Remembrance Day, I always conclude with the poem, <u>We Remember Them.</u> Even at one of my granddaughter's Bas Mitzvah ceremony, she read this poem. At this completion of my story, I would like to end with it.

<u>We Remember Them</u>

At the rising of the sun and its going down,
> WE REMEMBER THEM.

At the blowing of the wind and in the chill of the winter,
> WE REMEMBER THEM.

At the opening of the buds and in the rebirth of spring,
> WE REMEMBER THEM

At the blueness of the sky and in the warmth of the summer,
> WE REMEMBER THEM

At the rustling of the leaves, and the beauty of autumn,
> WE REMEMBER THEM

At the beginning of the year and when it ends,
> WE REMEMBER THEM

As long as we live, they too will live for they are now a part of as
> WE REMEMBER THEM

When we are weary and in need of strength,
> WE REMEMBER THEM

When we are lost and sick at heart,
> WE REMEMBER THEM

When we have joy we crave to share,
> WE REMEMBER THEM

When we have decisions that are difficult to make,
> WE REMEMBER THEM

When we have achievements that are based on theirs,
> WE REMEMBER THEM

As long as we live, they too will live; for they are now a part of us as

WE REMEMBER THEM

This poem was written by a Holocaust Survivor from my home town. She was 11 years old in 1939 when the Nazis invaded Poland.

A Holocaust Child by Miriam Somer

A Holocaust child is a child who's eyes reflect horror and pain. A child who's eyes ask "why?" Why have I been chosen, singled out to experience unspeakable agony from the hand of cruel tyranny.

A Holocaust child is a child who learned that being Jewish is a crime punishable by death.

A child who asked his mother "why?" Why did you bring me into a world when a child cannot have hope, that one day he too will be able to play, sing and even dream those ordinary dreams that carefree children dream.

A Holocaust child is a child who has experienced absolute evil. Who has been torn out from his mother's loving arms. Who was forced to watch the hanging or shootings of his mother, father, sister or brother.

A Holocaust child is begging, in the name of God, don't let us forget the Holocaust.

Take an active stand to those who are denying there ever was a Holocaust.

These words were written by General Dwight D. Eisenhower who helped liberate Ohrdruf, one of Buchenwald's camps in Germany. He later became the 34th President of the United States of America:

"The things I saw beggar description The visual evidence and the verbal testimony of starvation, cruelty, and bestiality were so overpowering as to leave me a bit sick... I made the visit deliberately, in order to be in a position to give firsthand evidence of these things if ever, in the future, there develops a tendency to charge these allegations merely to "propaganda"

--General Dwight D. Eisenhower
April 12, 1945

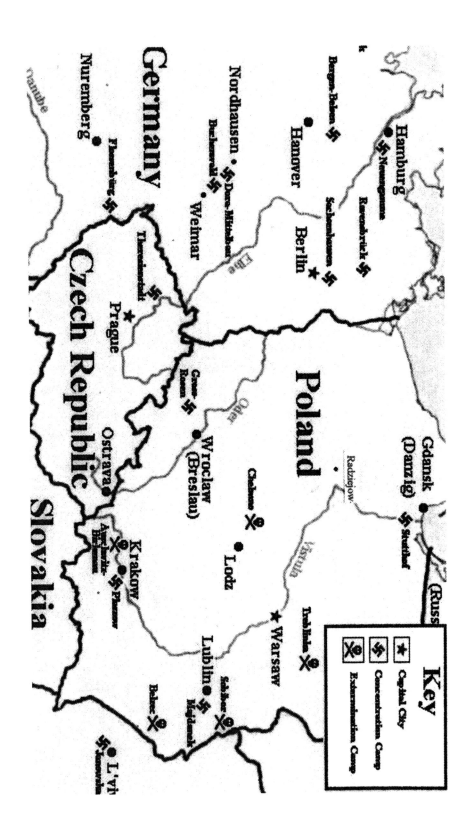

CPSIA information can be obtained
at www.ICGtesting.com
Printed in the USA
FFOW03n2311020517
35217FF